AN ILLUSTRATED GUIDE TO
WEAPONS OF THE MODERN
SOVIET
GROUND FORCES

a Salamander book

Published by Arco Publishing, Inc.
NEW YORK

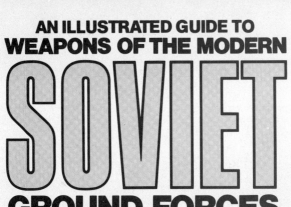

AN ILLUSTRATED GUIDE TO
WEAPONS OF THE MODERN
SOVIET
GROUND FORCES

Edited by
Ray Bonds

A Salamander Book

Published by Arco Publishing Inc.,
219 Park Avenue South, New York, N.Y. 10003, United States of America.
© 1981 Salamander Books Ltd., Salamander House,
27 Old Gloucester Street, London WC1N 3AF, United Kingdom.
All rights reserved.
ISBN 0-668-05344-5 Library of Congress catalog card number 81-67085
All correspondence concerning the content of this volume should be addressed
to Salamander Books Ltd.
This book may not be sold outside the United States of America and Canada.

Contents

Credits

Editor: Ray Bonds
Designer: Barry Savage
Color drawings:
Terry Hadler and J. Wood & Associates
(© Salamander Books Ltd.); and
(pages 38-39, 44-45) © Profile
Publications Ltd.
Printed: in Belgium by
Henri Proost et Cie.

Photographs: The publishers wish to
thank all the official international
government archives (especially the
British Ministry of Defence and the US
Department of Defense), Novosti and
Tass and the private collections and
other organisations who have supplied
photographs for this book.

Organisation of the Soviet Ground Forces

One of the basic tenets of Soviet tactical doctrine is that the offensive is the only practicable form of

THE ROLE of the Communist Party of the Soviet Union (CPSU) is to guide and direct Soviet society along the road to communism. In fulfilment of what it believes to be a historic mission, the Communist Party feels obliged to exert control over all aspects of human behaviour. Every branch of Soviet society is subject to the direction and supervision of the CPSU, and the armed forces are obviously no exception. Indeed, because they constitute the party's main instrument for controlling Soviet society as a whole, yet are at the same time the only organisation within that society which could ever succeed in overthrowing the dictatorship of the party, the armed forces are singled out for especially thorough political control and supervision.

The brain of an army can usually be found in its General Staff, and this applies particularly to the Soviet Army which has a very strong staff system. Nevertheless, the CPSU can justifiably claim to be the Soviet Army's central nervous system and animating spirit. Moreover, it is precisely because the CPSU fulfils this same function in the whole of Soviet society that the term Soviet "war machine" has real meaning.

By inserting party members into every social institution at all levels, and by ensuring that professional promotion relies on party approval, the CPSU contrives to achieve a unity of aim and purpose—albeit enforced—in Soviet society which is rarely to be found in the West.

Because Marxist ideology insists that the hostile capitalist West will

——— Military District boundaries

seek to destroy the Soviet state and end the rule of the Communist Party (and the history of the USSR over the past 70 years tends to reinforce this belief in the minds of Soviet citizens), it is hardly surprising that the party has made use of its position of power during this time to prepare the Soviet economy and people for war. While it is difficult to reach a precise figure, many Western specialists would agree that a good third of all public warfare for the Soviet Union, and everything about the army—tactics, organisation, equipment—is designed with this in view. The Soviet ground forces are far more powerful than is necessary to deter NATO from invading Russia and may be sufficient, given the right circumstances, to invade Western Europe, defeat the forces of NATO and bring most of Western Europe under Soviet domination. The purpose of this guide is to show and describe in detail the major weaponry and equipment of the modern Soviet Army, with the exception of helicopters which can be found in a companion volume.

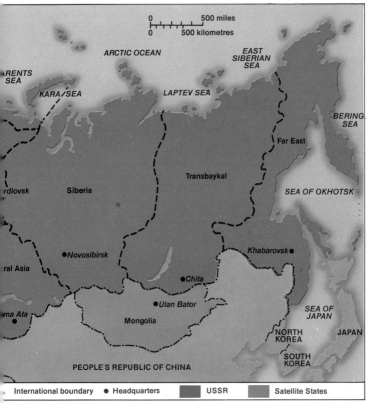

expenditure and resources in the Soviet Union is earmarked for arms. What is more, the characteristics of the Soviet system mean that it is far easier to divert resources into defence projects than it would be in a Western society.

The Ground Forces

The Soviet Ground Forces constitute a separate arm of service in the Soviet Union, second in importance only to the Strategic

Above: The USSR is divided in peacetime into 16 "Military Districts", each of which has wide-ranging responsibilities. Outside the USSR the organisations are different. Soviet forces in Eastern Europe are divided into "Groups", while there are autonomous commands in Afghanistan and Mongolia. In war "Theatres of War", "Theatres of Combat Action" and "Fronts" are formed.

Above: The Soviet Army has the services of some excellent designers, as witnessed by this formidable helicopter—the Hind-D.

Rocket Forces. Troops making up the Ground Forces fall into four categories:

Teeth arms—
motor-rifle (motorised infantry), tank and airborne troops;

Artillery—
missile troops, air-defence and field artillery;

Special troops—
engineer, signals and chemical troops;

Rear services—
transport, medical, traffic control, police, and so on.

A division is the basic all-arms formation, of which there are three types: motor-rifle, tank and airborne. The basic unit of the Soviet Ground Forces is the regiment, which is made up of three or four battalions plus support elements.

Battalion Organisation

The motor-rifle battalion's teeth are its three companies, each of three platoons, each of three sections, a section travelling in an armoured personnel carrier (APC). Artillery support is provided by six 120mm mortars and, in battalions not equipped with the BMP (which carries an anti-tank missile on each vehicle), an anti-tank platoon

of two recoilless anti-tank guns and anti-tank guided weapons (ATGWs). Logistics support is contained in a "tail" of only 15 or 16 vehicles.

A tank battalion is organised on similar lines, but has no mortars or anti-tank support, and has a slightly larger "tail". Tank platoons in the tank battalions of a tank regiment have ten tanks per company (31 per battalion) whereas motor-rifle regiments have four tanks per platoon (40 per battalion).

Regimental Organisation

The basis of a motor-rifle regiment is three motor-rifle battalions plus one tank battalion of 40 tanks. In addition a regiment has strong support elements including a reconnaissance company. Total strength is some 2,180 all ranks.

A tank regiment is considerably smaller, with 1,300 officers and men. Its basis is three tank battalions, 95 tanks in all. In the past, tank regiments had no organic motor-rifle troops, but front-line units now include at least a company, and in some cases a battalion, of motor-rifle troops. Artillery sup-

Soviet Ground Forces Weapons

Total armed forces: Active 4.1 million; reserve 9 million.
Ground Forces Command: 1.9 million active regular and conscripted troops (KGB troops 375,000, including border guards, Ministry of Interior troops 200,000, Construction troops 250,000). The USSR is divided into 16 Military Districts and Soviet troops abroad are formed into 4 'groups of forces'. In peacetime, teeth arms are organised in divisions of 3 types: 119 Motor Rifle Divisions; 46 Tank Divisions; 8 Airborne Divisions.

There are 3 stages of combat readiness
First category
over 75 per cent manned with full equipment scales
Second category
50-75 per cent manned with full scales of fighting vehicles but not necessarily of the latest type
Third category
10–30 per cent manned with 30–50 per cent equipment scales plus 'mothballed' obsolescent equipment.
First category equipment scales
Tank Divs: 325 tanks; 170 combat APC; 98 battle reconnaissance vehicles; 96 guns, rocket launcher vehicles or heavy mortars, plus
60 AA missile vehicles or radar controlled gun systems; 4 FFR (FROGs); 81 heavy anti-tank weapons.
Motor Rifle Divs: 266 tanks; up to 372 combat APCs; 125 battle reconnaissance vehicles; 144 field guns; rocket launcher vehicles or heavy mortars; 60 AA missile vehicles or radar-controlled gun systems; 4 FFR (Frogs); 81 heavy anti-tank weapons.
Airborne Divs: 102 BMD combat vehicles; 30 ASU-85 SP guns; 36 field guns; 15 battle reconnaissance vehicles.
Second category equipment scales
Tank Divs: 310 tanks, less AA defence.
Motor Rifle Divs: 215 tanks; 312 combat APCs; less AA and anti-tank weapons.
Third category equipment scales
These vary to accommodate stockpiling requirements. Combat ready vehicles usually comprise 75 per cent of Second Category scales.

Major weapons and equipment		*Estimated Totals*
Tanks:	T-72, T-64, T-62, T-55, T-54, T-10	44,000
APCs and MICVs	BMP, BMD, PT-76, BRDM, BTR-60, BTR-70, BTR-152, MT-LB	60,000+
Artillery:	152 and 122mm SP guns, 180mm, 152mm, 130mm, 122mm field guns; 122mm, 140mm, 200mm, 240mm, multi-barrelled rocket launchers;	20,000+
	120mm, 160mm, 240mm, heavy mortars, Spigot, Spandrel, Spiral	8 to 10,000
	57mm, 73mm, 82mm, 85mm, 100mm, 107mm anti-tank guns and Snapper, Sagger and Swatter anti-tank guided weapons.	
AA Artillery:	23mm, 57mm, towed AA guns; ZSU-23-4 AA SP guns; 85mm, 100mm, 130mm emplaced guns; SA-7 (hand held), SA-4, SA-6, SA-7, SA-8, SA-9, SA-11 mobile AA missiles.	6 to 7,000 (excluding SA-7)

Per annum production rates (USSR only)
Tanks 2,600   Artillery 1,400   APC/MICV 3,700

Frontal Aviation (Under Ground Forces control)
Helicopters: Hind, Hip, Hook, Hound (under Divisional and Army Control) 3,000+

Fixed wing Total: 6,000 aircraft: 1,000 fighters, 2,000 fighter bombers, 3,000 strike aircraft. Grouped in Tactical Air Armies, one with each of 12 border Military Districts and European Military Districts in USSR, and one with each Group of Forces abroad. Largest is 16 TAA with GSFG. Approx. 4,200 aircraft in Europe and European USSR and 1,800 in Central and Eastern USSR.

Aircraft types: MiG-25, MiG-27, MiG-23, Su-17/20, Su-24, MiG-21, Su-7, MiG-19, MiG-17, Yak-28, An-12.

port is notably absent; the tank regiment has only anti-aircraft weapons for protection (ZSU-23-4 and SA-9).

Both tank and motor-rifle regiments have engineer mine-clearing and river-crossing support, and decontaminating equipment. The light regimental tail provides scanty field recovery and repair facilities, and a small medical post as well as cargo and fuel vehicles to resupply the sub-units.

Division Organisation

The basic all-arms formation, the division, comprises three motor-rifle regiments and one tank regiment for motor-rifle divisions, and three tank regiments and one motor-rifle regiment for tank divisions. Recent increases in the numbers of tanks in motor-rifle regiments and divisions have, however, tended to make the motor-rifle division an equally balanced tank and infantry formation, while the tank division remains an armour-heavy formation. Both divisions have strong reconnaissance battalions with a "commando-type" parachute company for deep penetration; they also have effective battlefield radar and direction-finding equipment, as well as armoured vehicles for ground reconnaissance in conventional and nuclear war.

Motor-rifle and tank divisions have a considerable amount of artillery in addition to that held by their regiments, including anti-aircraft guns and missiles, towed and self-propelled howitzers, surface to surface missile and rocket-launchers.

A division has particularly strong mine-clearing and river-crossing support, much of the equipment having been proven in the Yom Kippur Israeli-Arab war of 1973. The engineers also have obstacle-creating ability using mine-laying vehicles and trench-diggers. Chemical defence troops provide good decontamination ability with personnel and vehicle decontaminating equipment.

The division's logistic tail is true to the principles of lightness and flexibility. The facilities of the technical support battalion are neither extensive nor are they designed for repairing heavily damaged vehicles. The medical battalion's field hospital is designed to treat 60 bed cases at a time, but provides light treatment or immediate evacuation for many more. The divisional supply transport battalion has the task of carrying fuel and supplies forward to the regiments. Divisional movement is controlled by a strong detachment of traffic police (the "Commandant's Service") who organise routes and deployment areas, site depots, and so on.

Military Districts

The USSR itself is divided in peace into Military Districts, which provide an administrative framework for raising, training and commanding military units, and the organisation and supply of military formations in a given territorial area. In peacetime the Military District is responsible for the garrisoning, training, and rear supply of forces; and also for military integration with the civil population, including Civil Defence organisations, pre-service training, conscription, military farms, etc. In wartime, the Military District is responsible for moving formations onto a war footing, transporting them to the

battlefront, supplying them and eventually replacing them with fresh forces. The importance of individual Military Districts depends mainly on their geographical location, which itself largely determines the level of forces maintained within them.

In the event of a war, formations of a Military District will be formed into groups of armies (Russian "FRONTY"). Several "FRONTY" in a given geographical area would constitute a Theatre of Combat Action (TVD). A Soviet TVD would be roughly comparable to, say, "AFCENT" or "AFNORTH" in NATO. Two or more TVD, and associated fleet(s) where appropriate, in a given geographical area, would constitute a Theatre of War.

Fronts
Soviet Ground Force formations, organised in peace into Groups of Forces outside the USSR, would in war be organised as "Fronts", and several Fronts would probably be combined into a "Theatre of Military Action". For example, the 21 Soviet divisions now forming the Group of Soviet Forces Germany (GSFG)

would probably become a Front in war, and along with the Northern (Poland) and Central (Czechoslovakia) Group of Forces, might be classed as the "Central European Theatre".

It is to the Front commander that the Soviet tactical air force (Front Aviation) would be subordinated. The Front commander would deploy his air power in coordination with his ground forces, allotting it to whichever sector of the battlefield he considered most important. The Front commander has in addition medium-range nuclear missiles (Shaddock and Scaleboard) which he can deploy as he wishes.

The airborne forces would also come under Front control; but, as a result of the limited amount of air transport available to drop or airland troops, and the great vulnerability of large-scale assault groups, the Front commander would probably detach a proportion of the airborne troops allotted to him to armies under his control.

A Soviet Front can have any number of armies, but in practice four or five would be about average. An army is likewise comprised of

Below left: The artillery has great hitting power, ranging from field guns to this SCUD-B.

Below: The USSR possesses more tanks than any other nation and is still building.

any number of divisions, but similarly, four would appear to be the norm nowadays. Armies with a preponderance of tank formations are known as "Tank Armies". Armies with a more even balance of tank and motor-rifle formations, or composed of a preponderance of motor-rifle formations, are called "Combined Arms Armies". The term "Shock Army" is a traditional title maintained for historical reasons. Military activity at front or army level is termed "operational", and the Russian word "operatsiya" (operation) is normally used in specific reference to army or Front.

The weapons of the Strategic Rocket Forces are employed for strategic (i.e., TVD or National) aims, but may on occasion be employed in support of a major operation to supplement the tactical and operational muscles of the Front Commanders. Although the airborne forces are organisationally part of the Ground Forces, in practice they too are strategic troops maintained under direct control of the Stavka. They can, of course, be subordinated to the TVD or front commander, if necessary.

Army Organisation

The organisation of a Soviet army is flexible, with a variable number of divisions of all types. A typical combination might be three tank divisions plus two motor-rifle divisions. An army disposes of a large amount of artillery, some of which in war would probably be retained for army use, with the balance being allocated to whichever divisions the army commander thought to be in most need of it. An army commander would be extremely unlikely to allot any of his medium-range SS-1C Scud nuclear missiles to a division. He would also have a tank reserve which could be used to strengthen an important axis, and a large amount of engineer equipment to construct more permanent river-crossing sites.

Most of the army's logistic capability is held at high level, because the supply of lower formations is the responsibility of the higher formation. In other words, the logistics tail of a division is not

Above: Virtually every army has discarded the flame thrower— but not that of the USSR.

there to keep the division supplied, but to furnish supplies down to that division's regiments and battalions; divisional supply is the responsibility of the army commander, and so on. Not only does this prevent division and lower units from being encumbered with large logistic tails, thus increasing their mobility, it also enables the army or Front commander to concentrate his supplies more easily on those axes where they will be of greatest value in the conflict.

Airborne Forces

Airborne forces are the elite of the Soviet Ground Forces. There are eight divisions, all stationed in the USSR as a strategic reserve of the High Command. They are considered the most reliable of the nation's troops, and are chosen to spearhead major operations, being used in this way in Czechoslovakia in 1968 and in Afghanistan in 1979/1980.

Soviet airborne forces are trained to operate in several roles. They could be dropped in small teams by advanced parachuting techniques

Above: Nobody could deny that the Soviet soldier is brave and resolute in the defence of his homeland. Whether he would be so determined in a war of foreign conquest is, however, not so sure.

to operate secretly as reconnaissance and sabotage groups in the enemy rear. Considerably larger units, up to a battalion or larger, might also be deployed deep in the enemy rear on special "suicide" missions of strategic importance, such as the destruction of a communications centre or government buildings in a city. Finally, they could be used in the traditional role, landed by aircraft, parachute or helicopter in the enemy rear to fight conventionally until relieved by the advancing main forces.

An airborne battalion is organised on similar lines to a motor-rifle battalion: three companies, mortars, anti-tank support and a light tail, although its equipment will vary depending on its role. The battalion is usually equipped with the BMD —the air-droppable infantry combat vehicle—which would give it a significant offensive capability and extra protection in an NBC environment. An airborne battalion group operating in the enemy rear would be quite a formidable force. It could be strengthened still further by helicopter-borne and air-landed

equipment, if local mastery of the air could be maintained and if, in the case of transport aeroplanes, a suitable landing field could be found.

The great increase in the number of helicopters in the Soviet Army in recent years gives commanders the capability to lift several battalion groups, with light scales, at a time, one particular advantage being that ordinary motor-rifle troops can be used with minimal training. This makes it more likely that helicopters would be deployed under divisional control to enable tactical operations to be conducted in close support of leading formations, and at very short notice. Equipping helicopters with heavy armament has enabled them to deliver heavy fire support to any landing operation.

Airborne forces, however transported, would have only a limited amount of supplies and ammunition, and could not be expected to operate without support or reinforcement for very long. The exception would be long range "diversionary" teams of up to 12 men dropped in the enemy rear to carry

13

out a mission of strategic importance, such as the sabotage of a vital installation or the assassination of an important person. Having completed their task, there might be no way for such groups to return or escape. This is their misfortune, as the strictly pragmatic Soviet High Command is not likely to worry about the loss of a few soldiers if they are able to accomplish a mission of sufficient importance.

Formidable though the airborne forces may appear, however, their role is only subsidiary to, and in support of, the operations of the motor-rifle and tank formations; for it is on the ground that the Soviets consider the war will be lost or won.

Roles of Ground Forces
The deployment of the Soviet Ground Forces leads to the conclusion that the High Command envisages two major roles for them, in addition to the responsibility for internal security in the Soviet Union and Eastern Europe which they share with the paramilitary troops of the Committee for State Security (KGB) and the Ministry of the Interior (MVD). First, they must defend the USSR from invasion by land from Western Europe, the

Middle East or China, and secondly, they must be capable of prosecuting a war beyond the Socialist bloc with the aim of extending Soviet communist influence to other countries. Close study of troop dispositions quickly shows that the force level which the Soviet High Command maintains facing China, while adequate to repel any Chinese invasion of the Asiatic USSR, is nothing like sufficient to ensure success in a major invasion of that country. The force level maintained in the European USSR and Eastern Europe, however, is much higher than necessary to deter NATO from invading Russia and may also be sufficient, under the right conditions, to invade Western Europe, defeat the forces of NATO and bring most of Western Europe under Soviet domination.

Military Doctrine
The principles of Soviet military doctrine, and therefore the shape and form of the Ground forces, are heavily influenced by the geography and economics of the USSR. The country is so vast and the population density (even in European Russia) so low, that the state simply could not bear the cost of fixed fortifications along its borders, even assuming that this

Above: Soviet military doctrine emphasises relentless offensive action after surprise attacks.

Left: Great effort has been devoted to building up air defences which will cover the advance.

kind of fortification could be made effective. Almost all of European USSR is a vast plain, bounded by the Baltic Sea to the north and the Black Sea to the south, while to the west the plain stretches unbroken to Holland. Eastwards, only the rolling hills of the southern Urals lie between Moscow and the Tien Shan mountains, where the border with China runs. Along her mountainous border with China the USSR has made an effort to create physical defensive lines in strength, because the nature of the ground and the composition of the potential enemy's army make static defence an attractive measure for deterrence, and for buying time in the event of attack.

The greatest obstacles to any military operations within the USSR are the massive size of the country and the large rivers which dissect it. Consequently, Soviet military thinking is bound to reckon with these factors, which affect attacker and defender alike, and plan the development of the Ground Forces accordingly.

The size of the Soviet armed forces in peacetime is limited only by the level of the Soviet economy. However, sufficient forces are maintained (a) to deter any possible attacker, (b) to provide sufficient strength for the USSR to repel any surprise attack and (c) to enable the USSR to launch (or to reply to) a surprise attack capable of achieving primary strategic objectives in the opening stages of a war.

An important consideration is that the 177 divisions of the Ground Forces maintained in peacetime are merely the framework of the Soviet Army. Only the "front-line" divisions in Eastern Europe, the strategically important airborne divisions, plus a very few elite divisions in the USSR, are maintained at full strength. All the others—three-quarters of the total —are maintained at half strength, or even cadre strength ($\frac{1}{3}$ to $\frac{1}{4}$ strength). The real basis of the Soviet Army's strength lies in its ability to mobilise reservists who have recently completed conscription service. Some 1,700,000 conscripts are demobilised into the reserves each year. These men can fill out the under-strength divisions and man the mothballed equipment comparatively quickly, bringing the strength of the Ground Forces up to over 5 million within a few weeks. It is the function of the Military District to accomplish this mobilisation, covertly if possible, although it seems improbable that such a massive operation could be achieved unnoticed by the West.

The Soviet Union's experience of being the victim of surprise attack, the geostrategic features of the country, the military assessment of the features of modern weaponry, and the national and ideological drive to spread her influence are factors which lead Soviet military doctrine to stress the absolute primacy of the offensive as a means of waging war. This lays great value on the seizure of the initiative, the ability to cover large distances at great speed and the achievement of the maximum of effect by manoeuvre, concentration and surprise, together with vigorous fighting to the very depths of the enemy's position. Thus, throughout these pages the reader will notice the ever-increasing emphasis on mobility, rapidity of movement, and the ability to concentrate or disperse quickly.

Main Battle Tanks

Despite all the developments of modern weapon technology, the Russians still consider the tank to be the most suitable instrument of their offensive. The Soviet commitment to the tank remains total, and much of their weapons systems development since the war has aimed at giving other arms the same mobility, protection and firepower that the tank forces possess. It is

---

T-72 Main Battle Tank

Combat weight: 39·3 tons (40,000kg).
Length: (Gun to front) 29·5ft (9·02m); (hull) 20·46ft (6·35m).
Width: 10·03ft (3·375m).
Height: (To cupola) 7·41ft (2·265m).
Engine: Water-cooled diesel of about 700bhp.
Armament: 125mm smoothbore gun firing fin-stabilised APFSDS and HEAT ammunition, with automatic loader; one 7·62mm coaxial machine-gun and one 12·7mm remote-controlled DShK AAMG.
Speed: 50mph (80km/h).
Range: 310 miles (500km).
Armour: Maximum about 120mm, possibly of modern "special" material resistant to shaped charges.

Below: The T-72 is now the principal MBT of the Soviet Army. It has a combat weight of 39·3 tons (40,000kg) and is powered by a 700bhp diesel engine. Hull and turret are of special armour.

recognised that today, on a battlefield saturated with guided weapons, the tank cannot survive alone, even in large numbers. Consequently all units and formations are to a greater or lesser extent composed of "combined arms" which afford each other mutual protection. This does not mean that all Soviet fighting formations tend towards the same composition, however. The Soviets still maintain tank-heavy formations, convinced that these formations are the best sort for rapid thrusts deep into the enemy's position, delivering a "shock" blow so as to precipitate his rapid military and political collapse.

Considerable confusion was caused in the West over the correct designation of the MBTs which followed the T-62. This was eventually resolved and it is now quite clear that there are two distinct designs: the T-64 and the T-72. The latter is a progressive development of the T-64, with revised suspension and a slightly different turret. It is also frequently suggested that T-72 may be constructed of a new type of armour, similar in concept to that developed in the United Kingdom and known as "Chobham armour". Should this be so, of course, it would mean that a large part of Nato's anti-tank armour could be negated, especially those projectiles and missiles equipped with a "hollow-charge" warhead.

The principal difference between T-72 and T-64 is that the newer tank has six large road-wheels, whereas T-64 has six rather small road-wheels which are quite unlike those on any other Soviet MBT. There may well also be internal differences between the two tanks, but this will not become apparent until examples of each become available for detailed examination by Western experts.

The T-72 is armed with a 125mm main gun, which is fitted with a fume extractor. The gun fires Armour-Piercing Fin-Stabilised Discarding Sabot (APFSDS), High Explosive (HE), or High Explosive Anti-Tank (HEAT)▶

▶ rounds and an Integrated Fire Control System (IFCS) is installed. The IFCS relieves both commander and gunner of some of their tasks as well as significantly increasing the probability of a first-round hit. An automatic loader is fitted and this, as with T-64, enables the crew to be reduced to three men.

This reduction in the number of crewmen is most significant as it has been strenuously resisted in Western armies, who do, of course, have a much more acute manpower problem than the Soviet Army. This means that the Soviets have been able to "save" 95 soldiers in every tank regiment, and this will have helped them to achieve the recent expansion of tank battalions in motor-rifle regiments from 31 to 40 MBTs.

T-72 was put into production in 1974 and entered service with the Soviet Army shortly afterwards. It is now in production in several State armament factories in the USSR, and is also being produced in Poland and Czechoslovakia. Current production is running at over 2,000 per year, which is sufficient to replace the entire tank fleets of both the British and French armies every year! All Soviet Army front-line divisions have now been re-equipped with this excellent MBT, and the other Warsaw Pact armies are in the process of putting it into service.

A special command version exists which carries additional communications equipment in place of the 12·7mm machine-gun. When stationary a 32ft (10m) mast can be erected. This version is designated T-72K. ▶

Above: A T-72 of the Tumansky Guards Division on parade in Red Square, Moscow. This picture shows the low, sleek outline of the tank to advantage. An infra-red light is fitted beside the barrel and there is another in front of the commander's hatch. The two boxes on the side of the turret contain ammunition for the anti-aircraft machine-gun. Note also the fuel tanks fitted into the track-guards; if the fuel is ignited due to a hit it will burn harmlessly without affecting the crew.

Left: A column of tanks moves forward escorted by its air defence: the SA-8 Gecko. The tanks are T-72s which have been specifically designed to fit in with the Soviet tactical concepts of rapid advance, early breakthrough of enemy defences, and penetration of the rear areas. However, tank columns such as this will need very strong air defences if they are to advance in line as they will offer very good targets to the increasingly effective NATO ground attack aircraft.

Above: A T-72 of the Tumansky Guards Division is inspected by French generals. The 125mm fin-stabilised ammunition is on display and the dozer blade can be clearly seen.

▶ Not satisfied with this tank the Soviet Army has had a new MBT under development since the early 1970s, known in the West as T-80. Current information is, not unnaturally, somewhat scanty, although most reports agree that the new tank is generally similar in size and shape to T-72, but with a slightly longer hull. The gun is probably the same, although it would be in line with previous Soviet practice to up-gun their next generation MBT, moving on to either 130mm, or even 152mm. The T-80 is certain to have some form of special armour, although whether this will be the same as on T-72 is a matter for conjecture. The USSR has been a world leader in metallurgy for many years and there is no reason why they should lag behind the West in new armours.

One of the most interesting features of Soviet tank design is the way in which they seem to be able to produce MBTs which excite the envy of Western soldiers for a combat weight some 30 per cent less than MBTs they use. T-72 weighs some 39·3 tons (40,000kg), while Leopard 2 is a massive 54 tons (55,000kg).

Above: A T-72 emerges from a river after an under-water crossing. This type of operation is essential to Soviet plans for a rapid advance across Western Europe, but is considered very hazardous by Western experts.

Left: This rear view of an early model T-72 again emphasises the uncluttered design. The large tube on the side of the turret is the schnorkel, which is shown mounted for river-crossing in the picture above.

T-64 Main Battle Tank

Combat weight: 39·3 tons (40,000kg).
Length: (Gun to front) 29·5ft (9·02m); (hull) 20·46ft (6·35m).
Width: 10·03ft (3·375m).
Height: (To cupola) 7·41ft (2·265m).
Engine: Water-cooled diesel. 700bhp.
Armament: 125mm smoothbore main gun, firing fin-stabilised APFSDS and HEAT ammunition; automatic loader. One 7·62mm coaxial machine-gun. One 12·7mm remote-controlled DShK AAMG.
Speed: 50mph (80km/h).
Range: 310 miles (500km).
Armour: Maximum about 120mm.

Western military commentators have suggested that the T-64 has proved to be less than satisfactory, and it is certainly true that the tank has not been exported on the scale of T-54/55, nor has it been produced in the Polish and Czechoslovakian tank factories. Nevertheless, it represents a major milestone in the development of Soviet MBTs.

A new experimental tank was running in the late 1960s which was designated M-1970 in the West; this mated the T-62 turret and gun to a new hull with six small road-wheels and return rollers. When this MBT first entered production as the T-64 it had the M-1970 hull and suspension, the 115mm smoothbore gun from the T-62, and a completely new turret and automatic loader. This latter device enabled the Soviet Army—to the great surprise of Western armies—to reduce the tank crew from the traditional four to three. A few years after entering service a modification programme was started in which the 115mm smoothbore gun was replaced by a new and even larger 125mm gun. New production vehicles, of course, were fitted with the new gun as standard. *continued* ▶

Below: The T-64 preceded the T-72 in production, but has only entered service with the Soviet Army. It has the same 125mm main gun as the T-72; the suspension is, however, quite different with six small road wheels of stamped metal. The 12·7mm machine-gun can be fired by remote-control from inside the turret.

Above: This view shows the infra-red searchlight fitted on the left of the main gun, and the AAMG ammunition boxes on the left of the turret; all are on the right of the T-72 turret.

▶ The 125mm gun is a smoothbore weapon, firing Armour-Piercing Fin-Stabilised Discarding Sabot (APFSDS), High Explosive Anti-Tank (HEAT), and High Explosive (HE) rounds. Forty rounds are carried, the normal mix being 12 APFSDS, 6 HEAT and 22 HE, although this can be varied in accordance with the tactical situation. The automatic loader enabled the Soviet Army to "save" one-quarter of its trained tank crews.

The engine and transmission are mounted at the rear of the vehicle, the engine being a new design of water-cooled diesel. Initial reports credited this with a power output of 1,000bhp, but a more realistic figure of 700 to 760hp is now generally accepted.

Despite its apparent lack of success, and its being superseded by the T-72, the T-64 has remained in production for many years, and some 600 are still being produced annually. It is probable, however, that the T-64 factories will be the first to convert to production of the new T-80. Many thousands of T-64s have been produced, but none of these seems to have gone to any of the non-Soviet armies in the Warsaw Pact.

One feature of the T-64 which has clearly been less than successful is the suspension. All Soviet medium tanks from T-34 onwards had used five road-wheels without any return rollers, so quite why the change was made to the very small road-wheels of T-64 is not immediately apparent, although it is known that the T-62 has a tendency to shed its tracks. The T-64 concept appears to have failed as T-72 employs a completely different system, while some modified T-62s have been seen with the T-72 style suspension.

Left: On this T-64 note the schnorkel tube stowed across the rear of the turret and the unditching beam at the back of the tank below the exhausts. The automatic loader on the 125mm main gun has enabled the Soviet Army to reduce the normal four-man crew to three.

Above: The formidable Hind-D combat helicopter is used to provide close air support to large formations of tanks, such as these T-64s. Note the close formations being used by the tanks.

Left: This view shows very clearly the sharp corner between the walls and top of the turret: one of the first indications to Western experts that T-64 might be constructed of "special" armour.

T-62 Main Battle Tank

Combat weight: (Fully stowed, no crew) 36·93 tons (37,500kg).
Length: (Gun to front) 30ft 8in (9488 or 9770mm); (gun to rear) 22ft (6705mm).
Width: 11ft (3352mm).
Height: 7ft 11in (2400mm).
Engine: V-2-62 vee-12 watercooled diesel, 700hp.
Armament: U-5TS 115mm smooth-bore gun, 40 rounds APFSDS, HEAT, HE, one 7·62mm (co-axial) with 2000 or 3500 rounds.
Speed: Up to 34mph (50km/h).
Range: Typically 310 miles (500km).
Armour: Up to 100mm, mantlet up to 170mm.

The I-62 was developed in the late 1950s as the successor to the earlier T-54/55 series, first being seen in public in 1965. It is very similar in appearance to the earlier MBT, but does, in fact, have a longer and wider hull giving a more even spacing between the road-wheels, a new turret and a much more powerful main gun, fitted with a bore evacuator. When it first entered service the T-62 did not have an anti-aircraft machine-gun, but in the early 1970s many were retrofitted with the standard 12·7mm DShK weapon which is mounted on the loader's cupola. T-62s thus fitted are designated T-62A. *continued* ▶

Above: The T-62 introduced the 115mm smoothbore main gun with its APFSDS ammunition. The tank itself, however, has not been an outstanding success and is being replaced by T-64 and T-72.

Below: Senior Lieutenant Yesaulkov (centre) with members of his tank platoon on training in the Siberian Military District. The characteristic Soviet tank suit is shown to advantage, together with the padded helmet. Note the absence of an AAMG on T-62s.

Above: These two T-62s are on training in the Siberian Military District. The 115mm main gun fires APFSDS, HEAT and HE ammunition and a total of 40 rounds can be carried. A stabiliser is fitted and the normal rate of fire is four rounds per minute.

▶ The main gun caused considerable surprise in the West as it appeared at a time when the majority of NATO armies had just decided to standardise on 105mm calibre. The Soviet 115mm gun was not only larger, but was also smooth-bore, a major departure from the accepted ideas at that time. The 115mm round is manually loaded, but once the gun has been fired it automatically returns to a set angle at which the empty cartridge case is ejected from the breech, after which it moves down a chute and is then thrown out through a small hatch in the rear of the turret. The tank has an average rate of fire of some four rounds per minute, and a stabiliser is fitted.

A "schnorkel" tube can be fitted on the loader's hatch, and is held upright by wire stays. With this device the T-62 can ford rivers to a depth of 18ft (5·486m), although even under the most ideal conditions this is a fairly hazardous undertaking. Very careful reconnaissance is required and the chosen crossing place must have good entrances and exits, as well as a firm bottom. Reports have reached the West from time to time of tank crews and even whole units refusing to take part in such exercises. Where Western tanks have been fitted for "schnorkelling" it has always involved a tube of sufficient diameter to enable the crew to escape through it. The Soviets, however, use a tube only some 2ft (61cm) in diameter through which there is no possibility of escape.   *continued* ▶

Below: A closed-down T-62 showing the small frontal area and well-rounded turret typical of all modern Soviet MBTs. T-62 is apparently the last Soviet MBT to have a four-man crew as subsequent tanks have been designed to manage with only three.

► From 1973 onwards, eight years after T-62 entered service, these tanks have been upgraded by fitting laser range-finders and a 12·7mm AAMG. In 1977 a much revised version was shown in Moscow fitted with six large road-wheels and return rollers similar to the T-72, but it is not known whether this was ever put into production.

The T-62 seems only to have been a success with the Soviet Army and the relatively few which served with other Warsaw Pact countries have now been withdrawn. It would seem, however, that despite this, and even with the appearance of the newer and better T-64 and T-72, the T-62 is still in limited production.

The main shortcomings of the T-62 are reported to be a poor gearbox, a tendency to shed its tracks, thin armour, vulnerable ammunition and fuel storage, and poor operating conditions for the crew. It would, however, be a mistake to over-estimate this last point as the average height of the Soviet soldier is rather less than that of his Western counterpart.

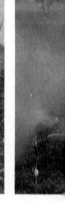

Top left: A T-62 on a realistic looking exercise. This picture shows the length of the main gun and the excellent ballistic shape of the turret. Tracks are, however, easily shed.

Bottom left: T-62s crossing a river during the Oder-Neisse exercises. Note the schnorkel, the hatch on the rear of the turret for ejecting spent cases and the long-range fuel tanks.

Bottom right: A closed down T-62 advancing as part of a tank/infantry combat team. The U-5TS main gun has an elevation of +17° and a depression of –4°. A 7·62mm PKT MG is also fitted.

Below: A platoon of T-62s advancing across open country. Formations such as this would offer ideal targets for NATO defenders but the Warsaw Pact has many thousand of tanks to be destroyed.

T-54/55 Main Battle Tank

Combat weight: (fully stowed, no crew): About 35·9 tons (36,500kg).
Length: (Gun to front) 29ft 7in (9020mm); (gun to rear) 21ft 7in (6570mm).
Width: 10ft 9½in (3265mm).
Height: 7ft 10in (2380mm).
Engine: T-54, V-2-54 vee-12 water-cooled diesel, 520hp; T-55, V-2-55 vee-12, 580hp.
Armament: D-10T, D-10TG or D-10T2S 100mm gun (T-54, 34 rounds, T-55, 43 rounds); 7·62mm SGMT or PKT machine gun (co-axial) with 3000 rounds; T-54 also one 12·7mm DShK with 500 rounds for AA use, and one 7·62mm SGMT (bow).
Speed: 30mph (48km/h).
Range: T-54, 250 miles (400km); T-55, 310 miles (500km).
Armour: Up to 100mm, mantlet up to 170mm.

The Soviet Army's T-34 medium tank is considered by most experts to have been the best all-round tank design of World War II and many are still in service with some of the smaller armies around the world. Some are believed still to be in reserve in the USSR, although whether this is for potential sales or for some use in a future war is not readily apparent. The first step in trying to replace this excellent tank was the T-44 which appeared towards the end of the war. If any production of T-44 took place it was on a very limited scale, and little has ever been heard of it. The next step resulted in the T-54 which did enter production and which has, in large measure, repeated the success of the T-34. No accurate production figures are ever likely to become available, but it seems probable that some 60,000 to 70,000 T-54s and T-55s were built, and these have served in at least 38 different armies.

The hull of the T-54 is of all-welded construction and the turret is cast, with the top then welded into position. The driver is seated at the front of the hull on the right, with the other three members in the turret. The commander and gunner are on the left with the loader on the right. The engine and transmission are in the rear, separated from the crew compartment by a bulkhead. The suspension consists of five road-wheels each side with the drive sprocket at the rear and the idler at the front. There are no return rollers as the top of the track rests on the tops of the road-wheels. The suspension is of the well-tried torsion-bar type. ***continued ▶***

Above: This early version of T-54 does not have a fume-extractor on the muzzle, but is still in service with the Warsaw Pact. The gun is 100mm D-10 with an elevation of +17° and a depression of –4°.

Left: A T-55 with its obsolescent 100mm gun. This weapon would have little effect on modern NATO MBTs except at very close range, but would still be effective against APCs and SP guns.

Below: Soviet Army T-54s seen in the suburbs of Prague during the invasion of Czechoslovakia in 1968. The policy of the USSR towards its neighbouring states is indistinguishable from that of Imperialist Russia.

►   Main armament is the 100mm D-10T rifled gun firing Armour-Piercing High Explosive (APHE), High Explosive Anti-Tank (HEAT) or HE rounds. Thirty-four 100mm rounds can be carried, the mix depending upon the tactical situation. Most T-54 and T-55 tanks now have a full range of night-vision devices and retrofitting programmes are constantly bringing the tank up to date.

There are at least five models of the T-54, differing in minor detail. In 1960 there appeared the T-55 with many improvements over the T-54 including a more powerful 580bhp engine and increased ammunition stowage, but with no anti-aircraft armament, although this last was subsequently corrected by the fitting of the usual 12·7mm DShK AAMG. The basic T-54/T-55 chassis has been used as the basis for numerous specialised vehicles including armoured recovery vehicles, engineer vehicles, minelayers and bridges.

There are at least four different types of related armoured recovery vehicle, these being known as T-54T, T-54A-ARV, T-54B-ARV and T-54C ARV, respectively. The most common is the T-54T which has a spade at the rear, a platform for carrying spare tank components and a jib

Above: The main gun at the top of the picture shows the 23mm sub-calibre device fitted for training in order to reduce costs. These tanks and soldiers belong to the Polish Army.

Above centre: A column of T-55s advancing in close country. The schnorkel tube is stowed at the rear and long-range fuel tanks are fitted, which can be jettisoned when no longer required.

Above right: Traditional Soviet tactics took no account of undulations in terrain, only of obstacles or commanding features. Modern NATO anti-tank tactics are forcing a rethink.

Right: A T-55 crossing a PMP assault bridge. An infra-red searchlight is mounted beside the 100mm main gun, and the 12·7mm DShK anti-aircraft MG is mounted on the cupola.

crane. Two basic types of mine-clearing tank are in service, one being of the plough and the other of the roller types. Three bridgelayers are in service in the Soviet Army, with a further two having been produced in East Germany and Czechoslovakia. The latest variant to appear is the IMR Combat Engineer Tractor, which has a 'dozer blade mounted at the front of the hull and a hydraulically operated crane that can be traversed through 360 degrees. Components of the T-54 are also used in the ZSU-57-2 anti-aircraft tank, the ATS-59 tractor, and the PTS amphibian.

Although still in wide-scale service with the Soviet Army it is questionable as to how effective the T-54 and T-55 would be in a major theatre of war, such as against the NATO armies in Central Europe. Their armour is thin by modern standards, but above all the 100mm main gun would have little effect against sophisticated modern tanks such as Chieftain, Leopards 1 and 2, and the US Army's M1 Abrams. The T-54/T-55 would, however, still be effective in secondary theatres, or even in the main theatre as anti-APC weapons. Thus, despite being some 35 years old in conception these tanks are likely to remain in service with the Soviet Army for some years to come, and with other armies probably well into the next century.

T-10 Heavy Tank

Combat weight: (T-10M, no crew) 48·23 tons (49,000kg), 54 US tons.
Length: (Gun to front) 34ft 9in (10,490mm typical); (gun to rear) 23ft 1in (7400mm).
Width: 11ft 8in (3440mm).
Height: (Excl. AA gun) 7ft 5in (2260mm).
Engine: V-10 vee-12 water-cooled diesel, 700hp.
Armament: M-1955 122mm gun, 30 rounds; (T-10M) two 14·5mm KPV (co-axial and AA), 1,000 rounds; (T-10) two 12·7mm DShK, 1,000 rounds.
Speed: 26mph (42km/h).
Range: 155 miles (250km).
Armour: Up to 210mm.

The Joset Stalin series of World War II heavy tanks culminated in the T-10 which entered production in 1956, having the same engine as the JS-3 but a more powerful gun and much improved armour and layout. It is important to note that, although considered to be very large and heavy by the Soviet Army, the T-10 at 51·2 tons (52,000kg) is, in fact, lighter than the British Chieftain, German Leopard 2, and US M1 Abrams.

The first model to enter service was the T-10, armed with a 122mm main gun and 12·7mm DShK anti-aircraft and coaxial machine-guns. The T-10M was a further development with a number of major improvements to increase its combat effectiveness. The 12·7mm MGs were replaced by 14·5mm weapons and the main armament stabilised in both elevation and azimuth. Infra-red night-vision devices have also been fitted and a "schnorkel" is available, if required.

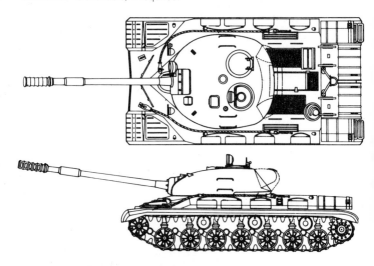

Left: The T-10M is fitted with a 14·5mm KPV anti-aircraft machine-gun which has a maximum range of 2000m and a cyclic rate of fire of 150 rounds per minute. Note also the infra-red searchlight on the cupola, and the smooth lines of the turret.

The 122mm gun has an elevation of +17 deg. and a depression of −3 deg., and 30 rounds of ammunition are carried. The T-10M fires three types of ammunition: Armour Piercing High Explosive (APHE), High Explosive Anti-Tank (HEAT) and HE. The APHE round will penetrate 7·3in (185mm) of armour at 1,092yds (1000m), while the HEAT round will penetrate 18in (460mm) at the same range.

Surprisingly, it appears that the Soviet Army still intends to use this tank to provide long-range anti-tank support, and possibly as the spearhead of an armoured thrust on a vital sector, where its very thick armour would provide protection. The T-10M does, however, have some shortcomings. First, it is slower than other Soviet MBTs, which would mean that other tanks might have to slow down to allow it to keep pace. Secondly, it has a poor depression on its main gun, making it difficult to use from reverse slopes in the anti-tank role. Thirdly, its ammunition is of the separate loading type, which reduces its rate of fire. Nevertheless its very thick armour could still make it the most difficult of the Soviet tanks to destroy.

Above: The T-10 first appeared at the November 1957 Moscow parade and has proved to be the last in a long line of Soviet "heavy" tanks although at 49 tonnes it is lighter than most Western tanks.

Left: This drawing of the T-10 emphasises the low silhouette.

Below: Rear view of T-10 heavy tank. It appears that the Soviet Army still uses this elderly tank, probably as a tank-destroyer.

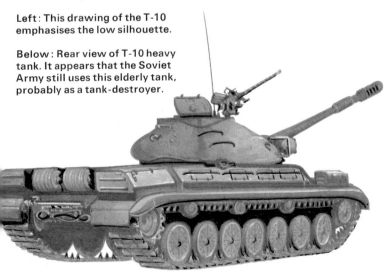

37

Reconnaissance Vehicles

Naturally, the Soviet Army fully appreciates the value of reconnaissance, and there is good reason to believe that much recce of possible routes in Western Europe has been done already. The field armies will, however, still need

---

PT-76 Amphibious Light Tank

Combat weight: (No crew) 13·78 tons (14,000kg).
Length: (Gun to front) 25ft 0in (7625mm).
Length: (Gun to rear) 22ft 7in (6910mm).
Width: 10ft 5in (3180mm).
Height: 7ft 5in (2260mm) (early models, 2195mm).
Engine: V-6 six-in-line water-cooled diesel, 240hp.
Armament: 76mm gun (D-56T, multi-slotted muzzle brake, PT-76-1; D-56TM, double-baffle, brake plus bore evacuator, Model II; unknown gun designation, plain barrel, Model III), 40 rounds; 7·62mm SGMT (co-axial), 1,000 rounds.
Speed: 27mph (44km/h) on land; 7mph (11km/h) on water.
Range: 155 miles (250km) on land, 62½ miles (100km) on water.
Armour: Usually 11 to 14mm.

Since it appeared in 1952 this large, lightly armoured but highly mobile vehicle has appeared in at least 15 different guises, and been built in very large numbers. The basic PT-76 (PT-76B when fitted with stabilized gun) is still the most numerous reconnaissance tank of the Warsaw Pact armies. To swim, the twin hydrojets at the rear are uncovered and clutched-in, and a trim board is folded down at the front. Smokelaying equipment is standard.

Its basic design of chassis is used in the ASU-85, SA-6 Gainful SAM vehicle, BTR-50, FROG-2/-3/-4/-5. GSP bridger, M-1970, OT-62 APC, Pinguin, PVA and ZSU-23-4. In front-line Soviet divisions, the PT-76 is now almost completely replaced by a recce version of the BMP.

detailed intelligence as operations proceed and the information will be obtained by deep penetration patrols, air recce and by vehicle-borne units. Both tank and motor-rifle divisions have a recce battalion, while each tank and motor-rifle regiment has a recce company. Engineer units also conduct specialised recce. Another means of obtaining inmation on the enemy is by electronic surveillance (radio and radar monitoring) and the Soviet Army has a good capability in this field also. It must not be overlooked, however, that modern recce will produce so much information that there is now a problem in handling it all.

Below: The PT-76 light reconnaissance tank has served the Soviet Army for many years but is being replaced by a version of BMP.

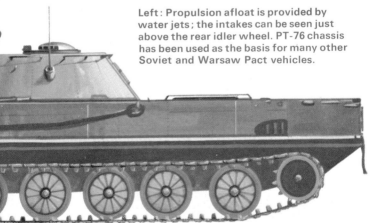

Left: Propulsion afloat is provided by water jets; the intakes can be seen just above the rear idler wheel. PT-76 chassis has been used as the basis for many other Soviet and Warsaw Pact vehicles.

BTR-40/BRDM-1 and BRDM-2 Recce Vehicles

Combat weight: -40, 5·2 tons (5300kg); -40P, 5·5 tons (5588kg); -40PB, 6·89 tons (7000kg).

Length: -40, 16ft 5in (5000mm); -40P, 18ft 8in (5700mm); -40PB, 18ft 10in (5750mm).

Width: -40, 6ft 3in (1900mm); -40P, 7ft 6in (2285mm); -40PB, 7ft 8½in (2350mm).

Height: -40, 5ft 8½in (1750mm); -40P, 6ft 3in (1900mm); -40PB, 7ft 7in (2310mm).

Engine: -40, GAZ-40, six-in-line water-cooled gasoline, 80hp; -40P, GAZ-40P, 90hp; -40PB, GAZ 41, vee-eight, 140hp.

Armament: Most, 7·62mm SGMB, 1,250 rounds; PB has 14·5mm KPVT turret, 500 rounds.

Speed: -40, 50mph (80km/h); -40P, land 50mph (80km/h), water 6mph (9km/h); -40PB, land 62mph (100km/h), water 6¼mph (10km/h).

Range: BTR-40, 404 miles (650km); -40P, 310 miles (500km); -40PB, 465 miles (750km).

Armour: All 10mm.

The standard reconnaissance vehicles in the Soviet Army in the early 1950s were the elderly BA-64 armoured car and the BTR-40, which had appeared in 1948. Both had major drawbacks in that they were not amphibious and ▶

Right: A closed-down BRDM-2 patrols a heavily rutted track in Western Russia. The turret is identical to that on BTR-60PB.

Right and below right: Two views of BRDM-2, which is sometimes also known as BTR-40PB or -40P2. Note the belly-wheels which can just be seen in the raised position in the lower side view.

Left: This version of the earlier BRDM-1 is a specialised NBC recce vehicle, BRDM-1rkh. Equipment includes an automatic flag dispenser above the rear nearside wheel; the flags are "shot" into the ground by a cartridge.

41

Above: This BRDM-1 has come under fire and is withdrawing under cover of smoke. Unlike some Western armies the USSR has never lost faith in wheeled reconnaissance vehicles.

Below: Officers of a Guards division reconnaissance battalion with their BRDM-2 scout vehicles. Turret-mounted machine-gun is a 14·5mm KPVT with a coaxial 7·62mm PKT machine-gun to its left.

►they lacked an adequate cross-country performance; this made them quite unsatisfactory to the army commanders as they did not fit in with their tactical concepts. In the late 1950s, therefore, a new vehicle entered production: the BRDM-1, which was also designated BTR-40P. This vehicle has a hull of all-welded steel which provides protection from small-arms fire. All four wheels are powered and a central tyre-pressure regulation system is provided. One most unusual feature is that there are two belly-wheels on each side, which can be lowered by the driver when crossing rough country. The vehicle is fully amphibious, water propulsion being by a single water-jet in the rear of the hull. There are many versions, some carrying either Snapper, Swatter or Sagger anti-tank guided-weapons (ATGW). Other models include BRDM-U, a command vehicle, and BRDM-1rkh, which is used to mark lanes through NBC-contaminated areas.

In 1966 a further vehicle appeared, known variously as BRDM-2, BTR-40PB, or BTR-40P-2. This has a modified hull, a more powerful engine, a gun turret similar to that fitted on BTR-60PB, and a land-navigation system. Again, many different versions have been developed, including one armed with Sagger ATGW, and a new air defence vehicle mounting four launch-tubes for modified SA-7 Grail SAMs. A major difference between BRDM-1 and -2 is that the former has the engine in front and the crew compartment in the rear, while the latter has the crew in the front.

There are many thousands of both these types in service with the Soviet Army and with other Warsaw Pact nations. They will normally be found in the reconnaissance units at battalion, regiment and divisional level, with the -rkh versions serving in chemical recce companies.

APCs and Command Vehicles

As with their tanks, the Soviet Army has poured enormous resources into the development and production of a huge fleet of purpose-built, effective and rugged APCs. All these vehicles have been designed to provide the means to enable

BMP Mechanised Infantry Combat Vehicle

Weight: Empty, 11·32 tons (11,500kg); laden in combat, 12·5 tons (12,700kg).
Length: 22ft 2in (6750mm).
Width: 9ft 9in (2970mm).
Height: Over hull, 4ft 10in (1470mm); over turret IR light, 6ft 6in (1980mm).
Engine: V-6 six-in-line water-cooled diesel, 280hp.
Armament: 73mm smooth-bore gun, 40 rounds; AT-3 ("Sagger") ATGW launcher; 7·62PKT (co-axial), 1,000 rounds.
Speed: Land, 34mph (55km/h); deep snow, 25mph (40km/h); water 5mph (8km/h).
Range: 310 miles (500km).
Armour: Mainly 14mm.

When it was first seen by Western observers in 1967 the BMP was thought to be exactly what the West's own armies needed: a true Mechanised Infantry Combat Vehicle (MICV). It was significantly smaller than the West's own APCs, but with much greater firepower. The eight troops have multiple periscopes and can, at least in theory, fire on the move. There is a vehicle crew of three: commander (who is also commander of the dismounted infantry section), driver, and gunner. Both crew and passengers ▶

Below: This view of a BMP shows a vehicle used by the amphibious assault troops of the Polish Army. Note the finer bow of later production models and sleek lines of this excellent APC.

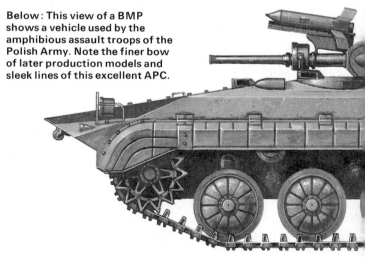

the infantry to move rapidly over the battlefield, keeping up with the tanks, and maintaining the inexorable advance across Western Europe. The BMP and BTR-60/70 are still leaders in their field, classic designs which have stood the test of time. The Soviet preoccupation with the rapid advance has also led to emphasis on command posts (CP) vehicles which can keep up with the pace of the battle. New CP vehicles are now being fielded to achieve this. In Western armies such CP vehicles are minimal modifications of standard APCs; in the Soviet Army they are custom-built for the job.

Above: The BMP is designed for rapid and mass exploitation of a breakthrough of a lightly defended point, in support of infantry.

Above: An assault river crossing. The BMPs have halted in the shallows and the troops have exited through roof hatches. The raised trim-boards stop water from washing up over the bow.

have nuclear/biological/chemical warfare protection in the pressurised hull, and air filters are fitted as standard.

The 73mm low-pressure gun has a smooth bore and fires fin-stabilised HEAT rounds, the automatic loader giving a firing rate of eight rounds per minute. The missile launcher above the gun carries one round ready to fire, and three more rounds are carried inside the vehicle. In addition, one of the infantrymen inside the vehicle normally carries an SA-7 Grail SAM.

The driver is seated at the front of the hull on the left, with the vehicle commander to his rear, the engine being mounted to the driver's right. BMP is fully amphibious, being propelled in the water by its tracks. A full range of night-vision equipment is fitted, although only the old-fashioned active infra-red types have been seen so far, which is, of course, easily detected on a modern battlefield.

A number of variants have been developed. One minor modification to the basic vehicle was that a sharper bow has been fitted to all versions appearing since 1970, clearly designed to improve the handling characteristics in water. In 1975 a variant was seen with the troop compartment replaced by a rear-mounted turret mounting a battlefield radar, known as BMP-SON no clear picture is yet available in the West. A reconnaissance version is now rapidly replacing the ageing PT-76. The radar version is armed with only a machine-gun; the recce version lacks an ATGW, but carries observation equipment as well as its 73mm gun in an enlarged turret. The recce version is designated BMP-R.

The Soviet Army received a rude shock when the BMP was used in combat for the first time in the 1973 Yom Kippur war. Used by the Egyptians exactly as taught in the Soviet tactical text-books the result frequently verged on disaster. It was demonstrated beyond doubt that the idea of a MICV which would charge onto enemy positions with all armament blazing away—including the infantrymen's rifles firing through ports—was

Below : BMPs usually follow the infantry in an assault; here they are leading, suggesting that this picture was taken before tactical doctrine was amended as a result of the Yom Kippur war.

very nice in theory, but totally unworkable in practice. There followed a very open, extremely frank, and valuable discussion in Soviet military journals, as a result of which the whole concept of the use of BMP was revised. Soviet doctrine now dictates that the normal use of APCs will involve the infantry dismounting some 220 to 330 yards (200 to 300m) short of the objective and completing the final phase of the assault on foot, covered by fire from artillery, tanks and the BMPs. It is, incidentally, interesting to note that the West learned a great deal from the Soviet discussions on the role of MICVs and APCs, and probably avoided some very expensive mistakes as a result!

A replacement for BMP is well overdue, their normal equipment cycle resulting in major types being superseded every ten years. There is no doubt, however, that the great tactical debate on the role of APCs has led to a slowing down of this process where the BMP replacement is concerned. Now that firm conclusions have been reached the APC design bureau is working on a vehicle which will be matched with the new teachings and compatible in performance with the new T-80 MBT. It had been thought at one time that the Soviets were producing so many BMPs that they intended to phase out wheeled APCs altogether, but the recent appearance of the BTR-70 eight-wheeled APC indicates that this is not so.

Despite the change in tactical use resulting from the Yom Kippur war there is no doubt that the BMP has been a tremendous success and today, some 15 years after its first appearance, it is still one of the most effective APCs in service with any army.

Right: Rather more typical of modern Soviet infantry tactics than those shown on page 47, the BMPs here follow the infantry in the assault. The 73mm low-pressure gun fires fin-stabilised HEAT rounds; an automatic loader gives a rate of fire of eight rounds per minute. The AT-3 anti-tank guided missile has a 6lb (2.72kg) HEAT warhead; three more rounds are carried in the vehicle, which have to be loaded manually through the gunner's hatch. Note the rifleman's periscope below the figure "6" and the firing-port in the side of the hull just above the track guard.

Inset right: BMPs advancing through snow. The demands of Soviet military doctrine and the realities of the Russian climate serve to ensure that Soviet equipment is well suited to winter warfare, and that the soldier is well practised in it. The BMP has now been in service for some 15 years, but a successor will soon appear.

Below: The new reconnaissance version of the BMP crossing a river. For some time this has been replacing the PT-76 in Soviet and Warsaw Pact armies. Note the trim-board and the more than adequate freeboard, which ensure good flotation. This is a Polish Army vehicle.

MT-LB Tracked Vehicle

Multi-role tracked vehicle.
Weight: (Empty) 11·71 tons (11,900kg).
Length: 21·17ft (6·454m).
Width: 9·35ft (2·85m).
Height: 6·12ft (1·865m).
Engine: YaMZ 238 V6-cylinder engine diesel, 240hp.
Armament: 7·62mm PKT machine-gun.
Speed: 38·2mph (61·5km/h).
Range: 248 miles (400km).

This vehicle was first seen in 1970 and was designated by the West as the "M-1970" APC. It is now known that the correct designation is "MT-LB". The hull is of all-welded steel construction with the engine between the crew and passenger compartments. There are two rear doors (as with BMP) and hatches over the passenger compartment. The sole vehicle weapon is one 7·62mm machine-gun, mounted in a turret identical to that on the BTR-60P. The vehicle is fully amphibious, being propelled in the water by its tracks. Although slightly shorter and narrower than the BMP, the MT-LB does, in fact, carry two more passengers.

It is of considerable interest that the Soviet Army has felt the need to develop another type of APC when it already had a superb vehicle available in the shape of the BMP. The MT-LB has not been produced in such large numbers as the BMP, although it is know to be in service with the Soviet and East German armies. Presumably, therefore, the Soviet Army wanted a less sophisticated and more adaptable vehicle, and considered that the additional expense of another development and production programme would be worth it in the long term. BMP has only been seen as an APC, command vehicle or radar vehicle, whereas the MT-LB serves as APC (3 crew plus 10 infantrymen), command vehicle, artillery command post, artillery tractor, cargo carrier, minelayer and radio vehicle. It is clearly a useful and versatile machine.

Above: The MT-LB is a versatile vehicle, being used as an APC, command-post, gun-tractor, cargo-carrier, minelayer and radio vehicle. These MT-LBs of the East German Army are towing T-12 100mm anti-tank guns, and are carrying the gun crews and first-line ammunition: self-contained anti-tank detachments.

Left: Soviet infantrymen having just debussed from their MT-LB. Although slightly smaller than the BMP, MT-LB carries two more men—3 crew and ten infantrymen. Armoured protection is, however, rather less and armament is confined to one 7·62mm MG.

Below: The four line drawings show the general arrangement of the MT-LB. The hull is of all-welded construction with twin rear doors and roof hatches. There is a firing-port in the rear door, and one on each side of the passenger compartment.

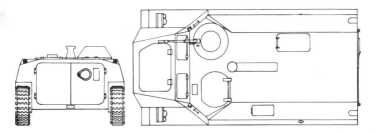

BTR-60
Amphibious Wheeled APC

Combat weight: Loaded: -60PK, 9·82 tons (9980kg); -60PB, 10·14 tons (10,300kg).
Length: 24ft 10in (7560mm).
Width: 9ft 3in (2818mm).
Height: -60PK, 6ft 9in (2055mm); -60PB, 7ft 7in (2310mm).
Engine: Two GAZ-49B six-in-line water-cooled gasoline, 90hp each.
Armament: See text.
Speed: Land, 50mph (80km/h); water, 6¼mph (10km/h).
Range: 310 miles (500km).
Armour: -60PK, 10mm; -60PB, 14mm.

First seen in November 1961, the BTR-60 family of armoured personnel carriers is impressive and is widely used in Warsaw Pact forces and has been exported to at least ten other countries. The large hull is boat-shaped for good swimming and to deflect hostile fire. It runs on eight land wheels, all powered and with power steering on the front four. Tyre pressures are centrally controlled at all times. The twin rear engines can be switched to drive waterjets. The basic BTR-60P has an open top or canvas hood, and carries two crew plus 16 troops. Typical armament is a 12·7mm and from one to three 7·62mm SGMB or PK. The BTR-60PK has an armoured roof, carries 16 passengers and has a single 12·7 or 7·62mm gun. The PB has a turret with co-axial 14·5mm KPVT and 7·62 PKT (the same turret as on the ▶

Right: The inside of a BTR-60PK. It all looks tranquil enough in this picture but, in reality, with 14 passengers on a long journey (especially cross-country) conditions would soon be most unpleasant. This picture illustrates one of the problems of the Soviet army with the three men on the right being of quite distinct ethnic types and speaking different languages.

Right: These Soviet Marines are landing from the original model of this APC, the BTR-60P. This has an open roof which leaves the passengers entirely without overhead cover. Sole armament on this example is a 12·7mm machine-gun. Automotive power is provided by two GAZ-49B water-cooled petrol engines, which are switched to drive water-jets in the amphibious role.

▶ BTR-40P-2) and carries 14 troops. There is a special version for platoon and other commanders, with extra communications (BTR-60PU). BTR-60P is the standard amphibious APC for the Soviet marines.

Following some doubt in the West as to the Soviet Army's intentions with wheeled APCs it is now known that a new design has entered service — the BTR-70. Like the BTR-60 this is an 8×8 design, and was first seen by Western observers at the November military parade in Moscow's Red Square. BTR-70 has a longer hull than BTR-60 with a redesigned engine compartment which changes the rear-end shape slightly. There is also a rather more marked gap between the front and rear pairs of the wheels. Apart from these differences, however, BTR-70 seems to be very similar to BTR-60PB, with the same turret and armament, although it is possible that the newer vehicle may have diesel engines in place of the two petrol engines in BTR-60. The unfortunate infantrymen still have to debus over the sides of the vehicle, a hazard which the Soviet Army appears to consider to be an acceptable risk.

Above: A BTR-60PB of the Soviet Naval Infantry coming ashore — note the Naval Infantry flash on the trim board. This version mounts a turret with a 14·5mm KPVT MG and coaxial 7·62mm PKT MG.

Below: A head-on view of a BTR-60 showing the low, squat attitude which is a major characteristic. The trim board is stowed below the bow and there is a good view of the suspension.

Below: A BTR-60PB driving past Soviet Marines undergoing training on an assault course. This version has an armoured roof and a simple conical turret mounting a 14·5mm machine-gun.

BTR-50
Amphibious Tracked APC

Combat weight: (Loaded) 14·27 tons (14,500kg).
Length: 23ft 3in (7080mm) (not 6910mm as commonly reported).
Width: 10ft 3in (3140mm).
Height: (Excl. gun) 6ft 6in (1980mm).
Engine: V-6 six-in-line water-cooled diesel, 240hp.
Armament: 7·62mm SGMB, 1,250 rounds (see text for variations).
Speed: Land, 27mph (44km/h); water 6¼mph (10km/h).
Range: Land 162 miles (260km).
Armour: Up to 10mm.

The BTR-50 was produced in some haste when the Soviet Army found an urgent need for a tracked APC to counter the first generation of Western APCs which began to reach field units in Central Europe in some numbers in the late 1950s. Based closely on the amphibious PT-76 chassis, the BTR-50 was first seen in 1957 in the open topped BTR-50P version. This vehicle could carry an infantry section, or artillery (usually 57, 76 or 85mm) which could actually be fired from the vehicle without the additional complication of off-loading. This open design left the infantry comparatively unprotected and an armoured roof version soon appeared (BTR-50PK); this gave some shelter, but made the task of dismounting somewhat complicated.

Normal load is two crew and 10 troops. Variants include the BTR-50PA with 14·5mm KVPT or ZPU-1 machine-gun, the BTR-50PU command vehicle with very elaborate navigation and communications equipment, and small numbers of special-purpose modifications used for such tasks as carrying ECM (electronic counter-measures) in front-line Soviet units. The BTR-50 has been replaced by the BMP in the Soviet Army forward divisions, but is still to be found in very large numbers in second-line units. It is also still in service with virtually all the other Warsaw Pact armies, although some use a somewhat modified—and rather better—version produced in Czechoslovakia as the OT-62.

The greatest shortcoming of the BTR-50 is that the passengers have no option but to debus over the sides of the vehicle as there are no doors. This would be a very hazardous operation under fire.

Above: The Czechs built a modified version of BTR-50PK designated OT-62, which has a higher road speed and range as well as a revised front compartment. This OT-62 is operated by amphibious assault troops of the Polish Army from a "Polnochniy" class LCT.

Below: This is the Soviet BTR-50PK. The major disadvantage of this hastily-conceived vehicle is that the passengers must debus through the roof hatches which makes them very vulnerable. Although replaced in front-line divisions by BMP, many thousands of BTR-50s remain in service with all Warsaw Pact armies.

ACRV-2 Command and Reconnaissance Vehicle

Combat weight: Loaded 13 tons (13·21 tonnes).
Length: 20·83ft (6·35m).
Width: 9·18ft (2·8m).
Height: 7·55ft (2·3m).
Engine: Model IZ-6, 6-cylinder diesel; 200hp.
Armament: Nil.
Speed: 34·2mph (55km/h).
Range: 248 miles (400km).

It has long been customary for Soviet commanders at regimental and divisional level to position themselves right forward, in a vantage point from which they can observe the essential parts of the battlefield. During an advance this has involved the hasty siting and construction of a chain of command posts, usually dug in, although rarely with overhead protection. This small headquarters comprises the commander, his artillery officer, an engineer, radio operators, and a tiny defence element. The detailed command of the regiment or division is exercised by the chief-of-staff, operating from a main headquarters somewhat further back.

This procedure is clearly most effective on the plains of western Russia where the terrain is open and flat, and visibility is excellent. In central and western Europe, however, the country is rolling, densely wooded in some places, and heavily urbanised in others. It is, therefore, debatable as to whether the Soviet commanders would achieve very much by being so far forward in the event of hostilities against NATO.

However, it is quite clear that they intend to try to operate in this fashion, and the latest evidence to this effect is the appearance of the ACRV-2, a large armoured command and reconnaissance vehicle.

No technical details of this interesting vehicle have yet been made public, but it is obviously based on the chassis used for the SA-4 (Ganef) surface-to-air guided-missile system. The ACRV-2 has seven road wheels with the engine and drive sprocket at the front of the vehicle. The driver and vehicle commander are right at the front, leaving a large compartment for the commander, his staff, and radio sets. On the roof is an observation cupola fitted with periscopes and an electronic viewing device.

The ACRV-2 is replacing the command versions of previous APCs: BTR-152, BTR-60PU and BTR-50PU, and illustrates the growing tendency in the Soviet Army to develop specialised vehicles, although an effort is made to utilise common components wherever possible. ACRV-2 also demonstrates the Soviet adherence to the philosophy of attack, with all current vehicles being highly mobile, amphibious, and with built-in nuclear/biological/chemical warfare protection.

These command vehicles play a crucial role in the headquarters deployment drills. Soviet HQs are usually sited near the principal axis of advance, with vehicles in groups. Photographs of Soviet forces on exercise suggest that the general standard of camouflage and concealment is mediocre, although this may be prompted by a theory that the HQ will move before any retaliatory strike can be made. The Commandant's Service which provides the route guides is also responsible for guarding HQs.

Soviet Army communications systems seem, in general, to be less sophisticated than those in the West. This is certainly not due to any lack in technical capability, and their very simplicity increases their chance of survival on the modern battlefield. Like most modern armies the Soviets constantly discuss cutting down on the size of their tactical headquarters, e.g., Front, division, but little ever seems to be actually achieved.

Below: Although it has now been in service for a number of years very few pictures have become available in the West of the ACRV-2 command vehicle. This vehicle is clearly designed to serve as a command post in the type of fast-moving attack which lies at the heart of all modern Soviet tactical doctrine.

Self-propelled Artillery

For many years the Soviet Army appeared to be the last major army in Europe to maintain belief in the value of the towed gun in a modern war. Then in the mid-1970s two excellent weapons systems— M-1973 152mm and M-1974

152mm M-1973 Self-propelled Gun

Weight: 24·6 tons (25,000kg).
Length: 25·52ft (7·78m).
Width: 10·49ft (3·2m).
Height: 8·92ft (2·72m).
Engine: Water-cooled diesel, 500hp.
Speed: 31mph (50km/h).
Armament: 152mm.
Elevation: −3° to +65°.
Traverse: 360°.
Projectile mass: (HE) 96·0lb (43·6kg).
Muzzle velocity: (HE) 2,149ft/sec (655m/sec).
Maximum range: 18,920 yards (17,300m).

The Soviet Union continued to use exclusively wheeled artillery for many years after Western armies had begun the process of converting to self-propelled weapons. This was somewhat surprising in view of the Soviet Army's doctrinal emphasis upon rapid and flowing advance, for which towed artillery is less than ideal. Nor can the innate conservatism of Soviet artillerymen be blamed, since they have been so innovative in other fields. ▶

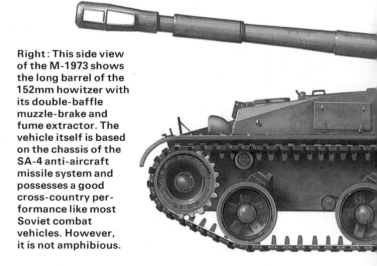

Right: This side view of the M-1973 shows the long barrel of the 152mm howitzer with its double-baffle muzzle-brake and fume extractor. The vehicle itself is based on the chassis of the SA-4 anti-aircraft missile system and possesses a good cross-country performance like most Soviet combat vehicles. However, it is not amphibious.

122mm—appeared, and since then they have been produced in great numbers. There are even rumours of a self-propelled 203mm gun, but these have yet to be substantiated. The well-documented Russian preoccupation with sheer size will, however, lead inevitably to bigger guns, as it has done in so many other fields. All Soviet tactical doctrine emphasises the over-riding importance of the attack and of fast moving advances. It also stresses the virtual inevitability of nuclear operations. The design of the SP guns so far revealed shows the implementation of this belief in offensive warfare.

Above: An M-1973 crossing a light tactical bridge. The advent of self-propelled weapons in the Soviet artillery confers a much greater degree of mobility on advancing divisions.

▶Whatever the reason, they are now making up for lost time and have produced two sturdy, effective and relatively uncomplicated self-propelled weapons, the 152mm M-1973 and the 122mm M-1974.

The first to appear was the M-1973, which was produced by taking the 152mm D-20 elevating mass, mounting it in a large turret, and utilising an existing chassis (which appears to be identical to that used by the SA-4 Ganef). The only noticeable modification is that the gun tube is fitted with a fume-extractor to keep the turret clear of toxic gases. Unlike the majority of Soviet AFVs, the M-1973 is not amphibious.

The M-1973 is being issued to the army on a scale of 18 per division, and it is believed that all first-echelon tank divisions have now been completely re-equipped. In addition, at least some motor rifle divisions also have the M-1973.

Main armament consists of a 152mm gun/howitzer which fires an HE projectile weighing 96·131lb (43·6kg) to a maximum range of 26,256yds (24,000m), but unconfirmed reports speak of a rocket assisted projectile with a range of 40,748yds (37,000m). In common with all other Soviet artillery weapons the M-1973 also has an anti-armour round; this weighs 107·6lb (48·8kg) which will penetrate 5in (130mm) of armour at 1,094yds (1,000m). A total of 40 rounds of ammunition are carried, and the normal maximum rate of fire is 4 rounds per minute; sustained rate is 2 rounds per minute.

A nuclear shell has been developed for this gun with a 0·2KT warhead and this represents a significant increase in Soviet artillery capability. Rumours concerning a 180mm or even 203mm SP gun have not yet been substantiated.

Left: A proud artilleryman salutes as his M-1973 passes the reviewing stand in Red Square. The gun fires HE, armour-piercing and chemical shells and has a maximum range of 26,256 yards (24,000m), but a rocket assisted shell may increase the range to 40,748 yards (37,000m). Reports of a nuclear round for this weapon have recently been confirmed.

Below: One of the clearest pictures yet published of the M-1973 152mm self-propelled howitzer; all the major characteristics of the design are apparent. Note the large muzzle-brake and the twin recuperators. It is somewhat unusual to find only one hatch in the turret roof. The 500bhp water-cooled diesel engine gives a speed of 31mph (50km/h).

122mm M-1974
Self-propelled Howitzer

Weight: 19·68 tons (20,000kg).
Length: 23·94ft (7·3m).
Width: 9·85ft (3·004m).
Height: 7·93ft (2·42m).
Engine: V-8, six-in-line, water-cooled diesel, 240hp.
Speed: 31mph (50km/h).
Armament: 122mm.
Elevation: −5° to +60° (approx).
Traverse: 360°
Projectile mass: (HE) 48lb (21·8kg)
Muzzle velocity: (HE) 2263ft/sec (690m/sec).
Maximum range: 16,732 yards (15,300m).

The second of the new range of SPs to appear was the 122mm M-1974.
This is also a straight-forward combination of the 122mm D-30 (qv)
elevating mass with a new turret, and mounted on a modified PT-76 chassis
(there is an additional roadwheel, making seven in all). ***continued*** ▶

**Above: M-1974s on parade in
Red Square, Moscow. The low
height of the turret implies an
automatic loader.**

Above: The M-1974 armed with a 122mm weapon. Here mechanics are examining the front-mounted Ya MZ-238 V-8 diesel engine; this develops 240bhp at 2,100rpm giving a top speed of 31mph.

Below: Main armament of the M-1974 is the 122mm gun, previously used in the D-30 wheeled howitzer (see pages 80-81). The chassis is a modified version of that used in the PT-76 reconnaissance tank (see pages 38-39). The vehicle is fully amphibious.

▶ The main armament consists of a modified version of the 122mm D-30 towed howitzer and is fitted with a double-baffle muzzle-brake and a fume extractor. This fires an HE projectile weighing 48·06lb (21·8kg) to a maximum range of 16,738yds (15,300m). The weapon can also fire a spin-stabilised HEAT projectile which has a range of 1,094yds (1,000m) and can penetrate 18in (460mm) of armour at an incidence of 0 degrees.

The turret is small and very low compared with Western SPs and it appears highly likely that an automatic loader is fitted. Forty rounds of ammunition are carried, normally a mixture of HE and anti-tank.

The M-1974 is fully amphibious, being propelled in the water by its tracks at a speed of 3mph (4·5km/hr) and, unlike many other Soviet amphibious AFVs, a trim vane is not fitted. The vehicle is also fitted with an NBC system.

The M-1974 is being issued to motor-rifle regiments to replace the towed 122mm D-30 howitzer.

Right. M-1974 122mm self-propelled howitzers of the Czecho-slovak Army on parade. The protuberance to the left of the engine hatch appears to be a filter and is only found on Czech versions.

Below: Virtually all Soviet Army divisions in Eastern Europe now have 18 122mm SP guns, adding significantly to their offensive capability. Despite their ballistic computers, however, batteries still tend to deploy in "line-abreast" formation.

Airborne Fire Support Vehicles

The Soviets believe deeply in the value of surprise, mobility, deep penetration and rapid exploitation, and this leads naturally to airborne assault (Vozdushny Desant) operations. There are eight airborne divisions in the

ASU-85
Airborne Assault Gun

Combat weight: Loaded 13·78 tons (14,000kg).
Length: (Gun horizontal ahead) 27ft 10in (8490mm).
Width: 9ft 2½in (2800mm)
Height: (Excl. IR etc.) 6ft 11in (2100mm).
Engine: V-6 six-in-line water-cooled diesel, 240hp.
Armament: Improved SD-44 85mm gun, 40 rounds; 7·62mm PKT (co-axial).
Speed: 27mph (44km/h).
Range: 162 miles (260km).
Armour: Up to 40mm.

One of the major requirements for an airborne force is to have its own fire support available "on-the-spot" and as soon as possible after the initial landings. The Soviet Army has paid particular attention to this requirement, producing a range of small, light and yet highly effective fire support vehicles such as the BMD, and the ASU-85 shown here.

Much heavier and tougher than the earlier ASU-57, this formidable vehicle became possible with the advent of the Mi-6 Hook and Mi-10 ▶

Soviet Army, elite forces at a high stage of training and readiness. So far as is practicable they use the same weapons and equipment as the rest of the army, but where necessary there is no hesitation in developing specialised items just for the parachute troops. The ASU-85 and BMD are good examples of this approach, being light in weight and combining heavy firepower with good mobility. Soviet airborne divisions are the spearhead of any Soviet foreign operation, having led the way into Hungary, Czecho-slovakia and Afghanistan; at least one such division is doubtless now on "stand-by" to go into Poland.

Top: Parachute troops leap off an ASU-85 to carry out a training assault. Carrying infantry on tanks is an old Soviet practice.

Above: The 85mm gun has a fume extractor and a double-baffle muzzle-brake. 40 rounds of HE, APHE and HVAP are carried.

Left: An ASU-85 emerging from an Antonov An-12 (Cub) transport aircraft. The vehicle is more of an assault gun than an anti-tank gun and 18 are held in each airborne division ASU battalion.

▶ Harke helicopters, and—for fixed-wing dropping—high-capacity, multi-chute and retrorocket systems. The ASU-85 was first seen in 1962 and is widely used by the Soviet, Polish and East German airborne divisions. The chassis is based on the ubiquitous PT-76, but is not amphibious. The gun has 12 degree traverse and fires up to 4 rounds per minute. A total of 40 rounds is carried, including HE, APHE and HVAP, giving the vehicle a capability against area targets, people, and armoured vehicles. It is believed that the ASU-85 is fitted with an NBC system. It also has various night-vision devices, although these are still of the active infra-red type; other target-acquisition and ranging aids may well have been retrofitted, however, in more recent programmes, thus upgrading the value of these neat and effective vehicles.

Another weapon developed specifically for the parachute forces is the RPU-14 140mm multiple rocket-launcher. This 16-tube weapon is used exclusively by the Airborne Troops, with 18 held in the artillery battalion of the airborne division. First seen in 1967, the launcher uses the same chassis as the M-1943 57mm anti-tank gun.

Below: ASU-85s drive away from the An-12 (Cub) aircraft. ASU-85 is air-portable, but, despite some reports, it is also capable of being dropped by parachute. The APHE round will penetrate 4in (102mm) of armour at 1,093 yards (1000m), while the HVAP round penetrates 5·12in (130mm) at the same range.

Top: Trained for any mission in every type of terrain and all climates, the 8 airborne divisions are the spearhead of the Soviet army. They are the first units to be employed in any major crisis, such as Czechoslovakia and Afghanistan. Note the infra-red searchlights on top of the main gun and commander's cupola.

Above: Paratroops "debussing" from an ASU-85. ASU is the acronym of *Aviadezantnaya Samochodnaya Ustanovka*, while the "85" refers to the size of the gun. Note that the paratroops are using the folding-butt version of the AK-47 7·62mm assault rifle.

BMD Air-Portable Fire Support Vehicle

Combat weight: (without crew) Estimated 8·86 tons (9000kg).
Length overall: 17ft 4½in (5300mm).
Width overall: 8ft 8in (2640mm).
Height overall: (excl. crew or aerials) 6ft 0in (1850mm).
Engine: Possibly a V-6, of about 280hp.
Armament: Turret identical to BMP, with 73mm low-pressure smooth-bore gun with auto-loading, from 30-round magazine, 7·62mm PKT co-axial, and "Sagger" missile on launch rail. In addition, two 7·62mm PKT in mounts in front corners of hull.
Speed: estimated at least 53mph (85km/h) on land, 6mph (10km/h) in water.
Cruising range: Estimated 250 miles (400km) on land.
Armour: Probably 20mm.

Two of the major requirements of a parachute-landed force are the ability to move small groups of men rapidly around the battlefield, and as strong an anti-tank defence as possible. The BMD is a very neat attempt to answer the first of these, and to add a reasonable contribution to the second. First seen in the November 1973 parade in Red Square this trim little air-droppable fire support vehicle is yet another of the "quart-in-a-pint-pot" designs which ▶

Above: Soviet Army paratroops on parade in Red Square, Moscow, on 7 November 1979. This versatile vehicle is the *Boyevaya Machina Desantnaya* (BMD), which combines the fire support role with an ability to carry six paratroops in an open compartment at the rear. The BMD is also amphibious using hydrojet propulsion. The turret is identical with that used on the BMP (see pages 44-49), mounting a 73mm low-pressure, smooth-bore gun with an AT-3 ("Sagger") missile above it. A unique feature, however, is that two 7·62mm PKT machine-guns are mounted in the front corners of the hull, one of which is clearly visible above.

Left: A Soviet airborne battalion with the ground mobility proffered by BMDs would be a great threat to NATO rear areas. Sufficient military transport exists to airdrop only one of the 8 airborne divisions at a time, but the Soviet civil airline —Aeroflot—is fully capable of air-landing operations. These BMDs are fully rigged for air-dropping.

73

Above: Soviet paratroops clearing a Dropping Zone (DZ) supported by a BMD. Such early fire support is vital to the success of a parachute operation; many have failed for lack of it.

▶seem to flow from the Soviet State arsenals. Though such aircraft as the Antonov An-22 (NATO codename "Cock") could easily carry the BMP APC, it was judged that the same capability could be built into a smaller and lighter APC capable of being airlifted in greater numbers, and more readily dropped by parachute.

At first styled "M-1970" in the West, the correct Soviet designation is "Boyevaya Mashina Desantnaya" (BMD). The vehicle has a crew of 3, and carries six parachute soldiers in open seats in the back. It is armed with the same turret as the much larger BMP, mounting a 73mm low-pressure gun, a 7·62mm coaxial machine-gun, and a "Sagger" ATGW on a launcher rail. One remarkable feature is the mounting of two fixed machine guns in the front corners of the hull. It is also fully amphibious, using hydrojet propulsion. It is a truly remarkable achievement to design all this capability into a vehicle weighing no more than 8·86 tons (9 tonnes).

BMDs were widely used in the Soviet invasion of Afghanistan and would be used in any major airborne operation. Its roles include bold reconnaissance immediately following a landing, rapid movement away from the DZs (especially to capture key targets), direct support of infantry assaults, and anti-tank defence.

Below: The compact design of the BMD is clearly shown. Soviet designers seem to be masters at packing great capability into small vehicles; this type has no equivalent in the West.

Towed Artillery

"Without effective suppression of the defender's anti-tank weapons no high speed advance can hope to succeed". Thus states the most authoritative Soviet tactician, and it is to the artillery that the main task of such suppression falls. To deal with the lines of fortification in the path of the advance Soviet gunners prefer a complex rolling barrage.

180mm S-23 Field Gun

Weight: Firing; 20·07 tons (21,450kg).
Length: Travelling, 34ft 5in (10,485mm).
Width: Travelling, 9ft 10in (2996mm).
Elevation: −2° to +50°'
Traverse: ±22°.
Projectile mass: (HE) 194lb (88kg).
Muzzle velocity: (HE) 2,600ft/sec (790m/sec).
Range: (HE) 33,245yds (30,400m).
Nuclear round: 0·2KT.

The S-23 gun is currently the largest piece of ordnance in the Soviet inventory. For several years it was thought to be 203mm calibre, but some examples were captured by the Israeli Army in 1973 and it was learnt that a mistake had been made and that they are actually 180mm. They are easily recognisable by their large size, the method of mobility with the barrel hauled back out of battery, and the pepper-pot muzzle-brake. The S-23 is towed by the large tracked artillery tractor designated AT-T.

Right: The S-23 gun was originally thought to be 203mm calibre, but in 1973 it was discovered that the correct answer was 180mm (7·08in). Like all Soviet artillery it has a very long range: 33,245yds (30,400m), and 47,900yds (43,800m) with rocket-assisted projectiles. Some confusion exists as to whether there is a nuclear shell for this gun; American reports state that the Soviets have a 203mm nuclear projectile—this may be for the S-23 or for a new 203mm SP gun which has been reported under development for some years. There are also reports that the Soviet Army has a 240mm nuclear self-propelled cannon, which must be a veritable giant, both difficult to move and to conceal. A possible use for Soviet nuclear artillery would be to break a deadlock should NATO forces manage to hold up a breakthrough operation.

When the defence is organised in a belt of strongpoints each of them will be engaged by concentrations of fire. There are three types of fire: preparatory (before the attack), supporting (during the attack), and accompanying (where guns travel with the attacking troops into the enemy rear areas). The artillery is also responsible for counter-battery fire and the bombardment of key targets deep within enemy positions. They are helped in this task by the exceptional ranges of all Soviet field artillery. Soviet towed weapons still have excellent performance, but are rapidly being replaced by self-propelled artillery.

As is usual with Soviet artillery it has a very good range (33,245 yards (30,400m), but this can be stretched even further by the use of a rocket assisted shell which has a maximum range of 47,900 yards (43,800m).

The S-23 is normally held in Frontal regiments, but, in line with normal Soviet practice, will then be allotted to one of the first echelon divisions.

There are three known projectiles. The HE shell weighs 88kg (194lb) and there is also a nuclear round with a 0·2KT yield. There is a concrete "block-buster" round, and it would seem logical, from known Soviet practice, that there should be a chemical shell as well. However, unlike virtually all other Soviet artillery there is not an anti-tank round for this gun. Rate of fire is approximately one round per minute.

As recorded elsewhere on these pages there has been a definite move in the Soviet Army in the past few years towards self-propelled artillery. Divisional artillery regiments are now virtually completely re-equipped with the M-1973 155mm SP and the M-1974 122mm SP. There have been rumours in the Western Press that the Soviet Army has started development of a 203mm SP, but it would seem more in line with previous practice if they were to take the quick and cheap method and mount the S-23 field gun on a self-propelled chassis.

152mm D-20 Gun-Howitzer

Weight: Firing 5·56 tons (565kg).
Length: Travelling 26ft 8½in (869mm).
Width: Travelling 7ft 8½in (2350mm).
Elevation: −5° to +45°.
Traverse: ±45°.
Projectile mass: (HE) 96·0lb (43·6kg).
Muzzle velocity: (HE) 2,149ft/sec (655m/sec).
Maximum range: 19,674yds (17,990m).

The standard heavy artillery of the Soviet Army, the D-20 is a powerful 6in (152mm) weapon which replaced the M-1937 (ML-20), also a 152mm weapon, which had served throughout World War II. The massive barrel has a large double-baffle muzzle brake, and a semi-automatic sliding-wedge breech giving a rate of fire up to 4 rounds per minute despite the use of separate-loading variable-charge case-type ammunition.

These gun/howitzers are usually found at Army level in regiments of 18 weapons; further regiments may also be found at "Front" level. These towed guns do not fit in with current Soviet Army tactical doctrine and are being progressively replaced by the self-propelled version. Among other Warsaw Pact armies Czechoslovakia, East Germany, Hungary and Romania are known to use the D-20.

Right: The 152mm D-20 gun-howitzer was introduced in 1955 to replace the 152mm M-1943 D-1 and is normally to be found in the artillery regiments at Front and Army level. It fires a 96lb (43·6kg) shell to a maximum range of 19,674yds (18km).

130mm M-46 Field Gun

Weight: Firing 7·57 tons (7700kg).
Length: (Travelling) 38·47ft (11·73m).
Width: (Travelling) 8·04ft (2·45m).
Elevation: −2·5° to +45°.
Traverse: 50°
Projectile mass: (HE) 73·6lb (33·4kg).
Muzzle velocity: (HE) 3,050ft/sec (930m/sec).
Maximum range: 29,700yds (27,150m).

There is no doubt that the Soviet artillery designers lead the world in producing simple, effective and reliable guns, with a greater range for a given calibre than any other nation seems to be able to achieve. Typical of the many excellent wheeled artillery pieces is the 130mm M-46, which first appeared publicly in 1954, and which is still one of the most powerful of its type in the world.

The M-46 is the only towed gun commonly used in Soviet Army field artillery units, all other weapons being howitzers. The M-46 is normally found at Front level where there are two battalions, each of 18 guns. Its main role is counter-battery fire, for which it has a high-explosive (HE) round weighing 74lb (33·6kg) with a maximum range of 29,691yds (27,150m). This performance can only be bettered in the West by the American 175mm M-107 and the new 155mm M-198 with a rocket-assisted shell. As with all other Soviet Army indirect-fire weapons the M-46 is also supplied with an anti-tank round (actually Armour Piercing High Explosive) which will penetrate 230mm of armour at 1,093 yards (1000m) range.

In common with many other Soviet artillery designs, this equipment is in service around the world, being used by some 17 armies.

Above: The 130mm M-46 was originally a naval gun, but was re-mounted for field use because of its exceptional range—29,700yds (27,150m). It is held at Army level for use in counter-bombardment and long-range engagements. It is in service with many armies and is also built in China as the Type 59. It is towed by a tracked tractor which also carries the crew of nine and the ammunition.

122mm D-30 Field Howitzer

Weight: Firing 3·1 tons (3150kg).
Length: Travelling 17ft 8½in (5400mm).
Width: Travelling 6ft 5in (1950mm).
Elevation: −7° to +70°.
Traverse: 360°.
Projectile mass: (HE) 48·1lb (21·8kg).
Muzzle velocity: (HE) 2,264ft/sec (690m/sec).
Maximum range: (HE) 16,732yds (15,300m).

This howitzer of 122mm (4·8in) calibre, typifies the dramatically advanced and effective design of the latest Soviet artillery. It is towed by a large lunette lug under or just behind the muzzle brake, with its trails folded under the barrel. To fire, the crew of seven rapidly unhitch, lower the central firing jack (lifting the wheels off the ground) and swing the outer trails through 120° on each side. The gun can then be aimed immediately to any point of the compass. The barrel is carried under a prominent recoil system, has a semi-auto vertically sliding wedge breechblock, and fires cased but variable-charge, separate-loading ammunition. The D-30 is the basic field gun of the Soviet Army, and is used throughout the Warsaw Pact. In addition to conventional or chemical shells, it fires a fin-stabilised non-rotating HEAT shell from its rifled barrel, giving it a formidable direct fire capability against armour.

Above: Soviet artillerymen bring D-30 122mm howitzers into action. The neat mounting enables the crew to change targets quickly and accurately. The breech is of the vertical, sliding-type, and is semi-automatic in operation.

Top: D-30s about to fire. The Soviet artillery persists in lining up its guns in rows of four in the open making a tempting target for both air attack and counter-battery engagements.

Above: A D-30 being brought into action. The central firing jack has been lowered and the three legs deployed. The crew are driving perforated metal stakes into the ends of the legs; all that remains is to pull the gun back into the firing position.

100mm M-1955 and T-12 Anti-tank and Field Guns

Weight: Firing 2·95 tons (3000kg).
Length: Travelling, 28ft 7in (8717mm).
Width: Travelling, 5ft 2½in (185mm).
Elevation: −10° to +20°
Traverse: ±14°.
Projectile mass: (APHE) 35lb (15·9kg).
Muzzle velocity: (APHE) 3,280ft/sec (1000m/sec).
Maximum range: (HE) 16,841yds (15,400).

One of the most widely used guns of the Warsaw Pact ground forces, these long-barreled (56 calibres) weapons have high muzzle velocity and can fire HE, APHE or HEAT ammunition. Fixed ammunition is used, which with the semi-automatic, vertical-sliding wedge breechblock gives a practical rate of fire of 7 to 8 rds/min. The M-1955 is lighter than the old M-1944 (D-10) and runs on single-tyres. It has box-section split trails, twin recoil cylinders behind the shield, and a prominent "pepperpot" muzzle brake. The later T-12, which has replaced the M-1955 in many Soviet and E. German units since 1968, is a smooth bore weapon firing fin-stabilised ammunition of much improved effectiveness. The most obvious difference is that the muzzle brake does not taper and is only fractionally larger in diameter than the barrel. Usual towing vehicle is the Zil-131, Zil-157 or AT-P tracked tug.

Top right: 100mm T-12 anti-tank gun. The USSR is virtually the only country still developing this traditional type of weapon.

Right: M-1955 100mm field guns were the predecessors of the T-12.

85mm D-44 and SD-44 Anti-tank and Field Guns

Length travelling: (D-44) 27ft 4in (8340mm); (SD-44) 27ft 0in (8220mm).
Width travelling: (Both) 5ft 10in (1780mm).
Elevation: (Both) −7° to +35°.
Traverse: ±27°.
Projectile mass: (HE) 21·0lb (9·5kg); (HVAP) 11·0lb (5kg).
Muzzle velocity: (HE) 2,598ft/sec (792m/sec); (HVAP) 3,379ft/sec (1030m/sec).
Maximum range: (HE) 17,114yds (15650m).

Variously designated D-44, D-48 or M-1945, the 85mm divisional gun is one of the most widely used by the Soviets. It fires various kinds of fixed ammunition at 15 to 20 rds/min, with the usual semi-automatic vertical-sliding wedge-type breech. The muzzle brake is a double baffle. To enable this gun to drive itself about the battlefield it can be fitted with an auxiliary engine, becoming the SD-44. The M-72 two-cylinder 14hp engine is mounted on the hollow left trail, in which is its fuel; the right trail carries ready-ammunition. The SD-44 has a driver's seat and steering on a large trail wheel.

Right: The D-44 gun uses the same barrel as the T-34 tank and is now only to be found in the anti-tank battery of parachute regiments. Shown here is the SD-44, which has a 14hp 2-cylinder engine mounted on the left leg of the trail.

Artillery Rockets and Missiles

For many years the Soviet Army has devoted much effort to the development of rockets and missiles, and it now possesses a variety of such weapons with an ever-increasing capability. Ranges are constantly increasing, while reaction

Frog-3 Artillery Rocket

Dimensions: Length 34ft 5½in (10·5m); diameter 15¾in (400mm); warhead diameter 21½in (550mm).
Launch weight: About 4,960lb (2250kg).
Range: About 25 miles (40km).

An acronym for "Free Rocket Over Ground", Frog refers to a family of unguided, spin-stabilised artillery rockets armed with nuclear, chemical or conventional HE warheads and intended to lay down a devastating blanket of fire on battlefield and rear-area deployments of troops and armour.
    Following Frog-1 and Frog-2, the oldest of the family believed still to be in service with Soviet and Warsaw Pact armies, Frog-3 was first seen in the 1960 parade and was the first to have tandem two-stage propulsion, each motor having a central nozzle surrounded by a ring of 12 smaller nozzles. At launch, both front and rear motors fire together, the front efflux being canted out to avoid destruction of the rear. The whole rocket impacts on target. Around 1970, Western literature agreed on a nuclear or conventional warhead weighing 551lb (250kg) but by 1975 this estimate had changed to a figure of 1,212lb (550kg). Carrier remains the PT-76 chassis.

Frog-4 Artillery Rocket

Launch-weight: Estimated at 4,409lb (2000kg).
Range: About 31 miles (50km).

This weapon system appears to differ from Frog-3 only in that the rocket has a slim warhead the same diameter as the motor tube.

Frog-5 Artillery Rocket

Dimensions: Length about 29ft 10½in (9·1m); diameter 21½in (550mm).
Launch weight: Estimated at 6,614lb (3000kg).
Range: About 34 miles (55km).

At first (1964) this was thought to be merely a Frog-4 with a conical nose. Later study showed that in fact the whole missile was increased in diameter to that of the Frog-3 warhead; in fact it is a fair guess that Frog-5 is a Frog-3 with a fatter but slightly shorter motor.

Right: On parade at the end of the Dvina exercises in 1970 are Frog-3s on tracked launchers, followed by the newer Frog-7s.

times and Circular Error Probable (CEP) are decreasing. In particular, the missile systems such as Scud, Scaleboard and SS-21 provide army commanders with the means to attack deep into enemy territory, both with conventional and with nuclear warheads. These weapons may also be be used for the rapid delivery of chemical weapons. While the missiles may be impressive the skill and the ingenuity of Soviet vehicle designers should not be overlooked. They have devised some remarkably capable vehicles (eg, the MAZ-533) which makes a significant contribution to the combat effectiveness of these weapons systems.

Above: Frog-3 unguided artillery missiles on the move. These elderly missiles are believed still to be in service; they carry either nuclear or conventional (HE) warheads.

Frog-7 Artillery Rocket

Dimensions: Length 29ft 6½in (9·0m); diameter 23·6in (600mm).
Launch weight: About 5,511lb (2500kg).
Range: 9·3 miles (15km) to 40·4 miles (65km).

FROG is the NATO acronym for "Free Rocket Over Ground" and is used to designate a series of tactical missiles starting with the FROG-1 which entered service in 1957. FROG-1 and -2 have long since left service, but FROG-3 is believed still to serve with some second echelon units. Mounted on a modified PT-76 chassis FROG-3 has a range of some 25 miles (40km) with a 992lb (250kg) warhead. FROG-4 and -5 differed mainly in the diameter of the missile, and may have had slightly greater ranges than the -3. FROG-6 is a dummy rocket used in training.

FROG-7 was the next in the series. First seen in 1967 it has—like all FROGs from -3 onwards—a central sustainer and a ring of 20 peripheral boost nozzles; there is, however, only one propulsion stage. The airframe is cleaner, the fins larger, and motor performance higher than previous missiles, while the launcher is simpler, with quicker elevation. There are thought to be speed brakes for range adjustment, but details of the necessary radar (doppler) tracking and radio command system are not known.

The carrier vehicle is the ZIL-135 wheeled prime mover, with an on-board crane for rapid reload. Cross-country performance is as good as the PT-76, except for the lack of an amphibious capability.

Successor to FROG-7 is the SS-21, which may already have been deployed in the Group of Soviet Forces Germany. No performance details have yet been published. FROGs (and presumably SS-21) are held in motor rifle division rocket battalions, which comprise two batteries each of two launchers.

Above: A Frog-7 battery of the East German Army on exercise. The sophisticated ZIL-135 transporter/erector vehicle is totally self-contained; note the jacks which have been lowered to give a stable launch platform. Between the two missiles is the GAZ-66 battery command-post.

Right: The excellent ZIL-135 TEL demonstrates its cross-country capability. A Soviet division has 4 of these launchers in 2 batteries, accompanied by 4 ZIL-135 resupply trucks each carrying 3 missiles. To the left of the missile is an on-board crane used for reloading.

Left: This picture clearly shows the uncluttered lines of the Frog-7 missile. The nuclear warhead has a yield of about 20KT and there is an HE warhead which was used in the Yom Kippur war, but with little success. There is also thought to to be a chemical warhead, but this is not confirmed.

SS-1 Scud-A and -B Medium Range Missiles

Dimensions: Length 36ft 11in (11·25m); diameter 33·5in (850mm).
Launch weight: Scud-A, about 12,125lb (5500kg); Scud-B 13,888lb (6370kg).
Range: Scud-A, about 50–93 miles (80–150km); Scud-B 100–175 miles (160–280km).

The Scud medium range missiles are battlefield support weapons designed to strike at targets such as marshalling areas, major storage dumps and airfields behind enemy lines. Warheads can be nuclear, chemical (persistent) or conventional HE. The original Scud-A version (first seen 1957) was thought to combine radio command of propulsion cutoff and gyro-stabilized guidance and to have not trajectory control after motor cutoff.

Scud-B is estimated to be 1ft 7½in (0·5m) longer and to have greater range (see data), and the propellant tanks appear to have been transposed. It was first seen in 1962 on the IS-3 chassis, with the steel-tube ladder round the tip of the missile suitably extended. In 1965 Scud-B made its appearance on the new MAZ-543 articulated eight-wheel prime mover, which is lighter and faster than the heavy tracked chassis. This carried a completely new erector/launcher much neater than that originally used. Soviet Ground Forces erector/launchers have numerous features not seen in the other Warsaw Pact Scud systems, probably betokening nuclear warheads which have not so far been permitted to other WP forces or export customers. The Scud-B erector/launcher is totally unlike that of Scud-A; there is

extensive new equipment, large double calipers to grip the upper end of the missile, and redesigned structure, but the prominent ladder that extended up each side of the earlier weapon to meet above its nose is absent. Guidance of Scud-B is by simple strapdown inertial system, steering as before via refractory vanes in the motor efflux, the fins being fixed. There does not seem to be any fine adjustment of cutoff velocity, and it is not known if the nuclear or conventional warhead separates before starting the free-fall ballistic trajectory. Resupply missiles are towed tail-first on an articulated trailer attached to a ZIL-157V, with a Ural-375 truck-mounted crane (Type 8T210) to swing the missile on to the lowered erector/launcher. Crews are trained to operate from points of maximum concealment, eg, heavily forested areas, to avoid detection. After a missile is fired the transporter is immediately driven to a new location to avoid a counterstrike and the vehicle is reloaded from the support vehicle. Certainly the time taken to set up and fire Scud-B is much less than the hour of Scud-A, and End Tray radar is used for radio-sonde (radio-equipped balloon) tracking for upper-atmosphere data.

SS-1C Scud-B is widely deployed by all WP armies, and by Egypt, Iraq, Libya and Syria. The Syrian Army was reported to have flown a Scud 155 miles (250km) in November 1975, but in the Yom Kippur war two years earlier three Scuds fired by Egypt all apparently missed their targets in Sinai. There are rumours of a Scud-C with range of 280 miles (450km).

Below: An SS-1 (Scud-B) on its MAZ-543 transporter/erector/launcher (TEL) vehicle. This is the basic Army and Front level nuclear missile and has a range of 100–175 miles (160–280km); yield is in the KT range. The weapon is designed to strike at targets such as major storage sites, marshalling areas and airfields. High explosive and chemical wearheads are also available.

SS-12 Medium Range Missile

Dimensions: Length 37ft 9in (11·5m); diameter 43in (1·1m).
Launch weight: Probably about 17,636lb (8000kg).
Warhead: 1×1MT nuclear.
Range: Estimated at up to 560 miles (900km).

First reported in Western literature in 1967, this mobile ballistic missile almost comes into the strategic category, because it can menace Western Europe from WP soil and is universally agreed to have a warhead in the megaton range. Yet in many ways it is similar to Scud-B; it is little different in length, rides on an erector/launcher mounted on an MAZ-543, and almost certainly has similar strapdown simplified inertial guidance. One of the few obvious differences, apart from the much greater missile diameter, is that the erector/launcher is in the form of a ribbed container, split into upper and lower halves, which protects the weapon from the weather while it is travelling. It is possibly shock-mounted, and the container may even offer limited protection against nuclear attack.

Though there are clear illustrations of the complete weapon system on the march, or elevating for firing, the missile itself remains almost unknown, and the data are little more than the best guesses of Western intelligence. It is reasonable to assume that there is a single rocket engine burning storable RFNA/UDMH. Steering may be by refractory jet-deflector vanes, but a later method would be desirable for maximum range. The Soviet Ground Forces enjoy a wealth of superb purpose-designed vehicles, and the

Above: An SS-12 is raised for launching. The MAZ-543 vehicle is a good example of transport design, containing the whole system and crew in one compact machine. SS-12 has been in service for some 15 years and its replacement is reported to be undergoing tests; it has been given the NATO designation SS-22.

MAZ-543 transporter/launcher is one of the best. A beautiful exercise in packaging, it is powerful, highly mobile on rough ground, air-conditioned for extremes of heat or cold, and has automatic regulation of tyre pressure from the driver's cab on the left side. The right front cab is the launch-control station, as in the Scud-B system. The rest of the launch crew sit in the second row of seats in line with the rear doors on each side. Some related vehicles are amphibious.

Like all Soviet tactical missiles Scaleboard is intended for "shoot and scoot" operation. But it is too large for snappy reloading and in any case this needs the services of one, if not two, additional vehicles. Resupply missiles are carried in their own ribbed casings, with propellant tanks empty, and even with fast pressurized-gas transfer the fuelling process must take about a quarter of an hour. The likelihood is that the Soviet Ground Forces already have a detailed itinerary of pre-surveyed firing sites offering good concealment throughout Western Europe. So far as is known, this powerful thermonuclear weapon serves only with the Soviet Union.

The successor to SS-12 is the SS-22 which has recently been deployed in East Germany and in the western Military Districts of the USSR. No pictures are yet available, but it is reported that SS-22 is more accurate than SS-12, with a longer range and more powerful warhead. It is also believed to be solid-fuelled.

Below: The SS-12 and its MAZ-543 transporter/launcher make a compact unit. The missile remains in its metal casing until it is in the vertical position ready for launching, and not one picture of the missile itself has ever been shown in the West.

122mm BM-21 Rocket Launche

Weight: One rocket, 101lb (45·9kg); launcher, 7,718lb (3500kg); vehicle, launcher and 40 rounds, 11·3 tons (11,500kg).
Length: Rocket 8·99ft (2740mm); vehicle, 24ft 1in (7350mm).
Calibre: 4·8in (122mm).
Engine: (Vehicle) ZIL-375 vee-8 gasoline, 175hp.
Speed: (Vehicle) 47mph (75km/h).
Launcher: Elevation 0° to +50°.
Traverse: ±120°.
Time to reload: 10 minutes.
Maximum range: (Rocket) over 16,395yds (15,000m).

An important multi-rocket system which first appeared in November 1964, the BM-21 uses a smaller-calibre rocket than any other of its era, and can thus fire a greater quantity (40). It is the first rocket system carried by the out-standing Ural-375 truck, which among other attributes has exceptional cross-country capability. The rockets are fired in salvo, or "rippled" in sequence or selected individually, always with the vehicle parked obliquely to the target to avoid blast damage to the unprotected cab. The BM-21 is used by the Soviet ground forces and by those of several other Warsaw Pact nations.

continued ▶

Above right: BM-21 rocket launcher battery firing. The rockets can be fired individually, in ripple as shown here, or in salvo. The effect at the receiving end is devastating, as each rocket warhead contains 41·9lb (19·0kg) of HE—a battery target could thus receive 4·78 tons (4560kg) in about 30 seconds!

Right: BM-21 battery preparing to fire. Note how the vehicle is parked obliquely to the line of fire, thus removing the need for any special protection of the driving cab. The vehicle is the Ural-375D, a sturdy and reliable vehicle with a good cross-country capability. As with virtually all modern Soviet vehicles there is a central tyre-pressure control system, to optimise performance.

Inset: The crew of a BM-21 receive their orders. It is com-paratively rare to see guns or rocket launchers set up in woods in this fashion, as the Soviet artillery seems to be unable to rid itself of the traditional habit of lining up its weapons in rows in the open.

► BM-21 is an especially significant asset to the Soviet artillery. Each launcher delivers its full 40 round salvo in less than 30 seconds producing 0·74 tons (760kg) of HE on the target. Reloading of the Soviet Army's BM-21 takes some 10 to 15 minutes, but the Czechoslovak Army has developed its own version carrying a palletised reload, which can load a second salvo in about one minute.

Multiple rocket launchers such as this can be used to bombard an area, delivering a devastating concentration of fire at critical moments in the battle. They are also particularly suitable for delivering chemical agents, and such projectiles are known to have been produced.

Above: The crew of an East German army BM-21 reloading their launcher. The Soviet version must be reloaded one rocket at a time. Czechoslovakia has developed its own version which comprises a BM-21 launcher mounted on a Tatra-813 8x8 truck. This carries a rack behind the cab containing 40 rockets; reload time is just 1-2 minutes.

Top left: An East German BM-21 crewman surveying in his vehicle.

Left: Five of the six BM-21s in a battery position. Tank and Motor Rifle divisions both have a Rocket Launcher battalion comprising three batteries, each of six launcher vehicles. Apart from HE the BM-21 is also effective as a means of delivering chemical warhead concentrations.

240mm BM-24 Rocket Launcher

Weight: one rocket 248lb (112·5kg); launcher, 5,995lb (2720kg); loaded launcher on ZIL-157, 9·35 tons (9500kg); loaded launcher on AT-S tractor; 15 tons (15,240kg).
Length: Rocket, 46½in (1180mm); ZIL truck, 22ft 4in (6800mm); AT-S tractor, 19ft 2½in (5870mm).
Calibre: 9·5in (240mm).
Elevation: 0° to +45°.
Traverse: ±105°
Maximum range: 11,000m.

The Soviet Union's 240mm rocket is a spin-stabilized weapon of relatively short and fat shape, packing a tremendous punch but having short range for its calibre. One of its standard carriers is the ZIL-157 truck, on which is mounted an open-frame launcher of welded steel tube, with two rows of six rounds. Another is the AT-S tracked vehicle, found chiefly in armoured units, on which is mounted a different 12-round launcher of the tube type.

Above: The BM-25 has long been a shadowy system, but this picture clearly shows these large rockets mounted in racks of five on the KrAZ-214 vehicle.

Above: The ZIL-157 truck is widely used in a variety of applications. It was replaced in production by the ZIL-131 in 1966.

250mm BM-25 Rocket Launcher

Weight: one rocket 1,000lb (455kg); loaded launcher on KrAZ-214 truck chassis 40,000lb (18,145kg).
Length: one rocket 19ft (5·822m); launcher on KrAZ-214 truck chassis 32·2ft (9·815m).
Calibre: 9·85in (250mm).
Elevation: 0° to 45°.
Traverse: 6°.
Time to reload: Not known.
Maximum range: 32,800yd (30,000m).

The 9·85in (250mm) BM-25 is the largest of the multiple rocket systems currently known to be in service with the Soviet Army. This system entered service in 1957 and is thought to be the first of the smaller rockets to be fitted with a liquid-fuelled motor. Its range of 32,800 yards (30km) is considerably greater than that of any other rocket system; the West German LARS, for example, is a 110mm rocket with a range of only 16,400 yards (15km). The BM-25 launcher has six launch rails, and is mounted on either a ZIL-157 truck chassis, or, in the case of the later versions, the KrAZ-214 chassis.

BM-25 battalions comprise three firing batteries, each of six launchers. As with other rocket launchers these are lined up in the open for firing, an old Soviet artillery practice which seems to indicated a degree of complacency, and which could be exploited by a modern and well-equipped enemy. Such a heavy and effective weapon will normally be kept under Front or Army command, although control could be delegated to divisions for a particular operation. The considerable payload of the BM-25 rocket makes it equally suitable for delivery of either HE or chemical warheads.

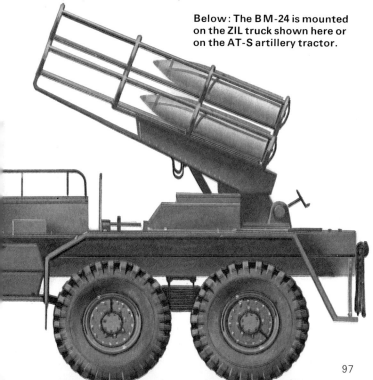

Below: The BM-24 is mounted on the ZIL truck shown here or on the AT-S artillery tractor.

Mortars

Mortars are a very effective means of bringing heavy fire to bear both rapidly and accurately, while their light weight and simplicity of operation make them ideal for the infantry. The Soviet Army has always been very keen on using mortars, employing them in vast numbers. They have also developed some very large calibre weapons,

---

82mm M-1937 Mortar

Weight: 121·3lb (55kg).
Weight: of projectile: HE 7·27lb (3·3kg); smoke 7·93lb (3·6kg).
Maximum range: 3,325yds (3040m).

The 82mm calibre mortar is widely used in Western armies, but only one model is found in the Soviet army—the M-1937 (42-43)—and that seems to be confined exclusively to parachute battalions. This is now very elderly, but it appears to offer satisfactory performance as no moves seem to be made to develop a replacement.

Below: The M-1937 82mm mortar has now been in service with the Soviet Army for over 40 years, and remains in service only with parachute battalions. There has been no sign of a successor.

including 160mm and even 240mm, whereas the maximum calibre found in Western armies is 120mm. These very large calibre mortars have such long barrels that the normal method of loading by dropping the bomb down the barrel cannot be used and the mortar must be "broken" like a shot-gun and the bomb inserted at the base of the tube. For some reason the Soviet Army does not seem to have followed the Western armies' practice of mounting mortars in APCs, as is done by the US Army with the M113 and the British with FV432, preferring instead to tow them on light wheeled chassis.

120mm M-1943 Mortar

Weight: Travelling 1,102lb (500kg); firing 606·3lb (275kg).
Weight of projectile: HE 34·2lb (15·5kg); smoke 35·3lb (16·0kg).
Maximum range: 6,233yds (5700m).

This very efficient weapon is found in a company of six in every motor rifle battalion and parachute regiment in the Soviet Army. It is mounted on wheels and has three types of bomb: HE, smoke and incendiary. The normal rate of fire is between 12 and 15 rounds per minute, but a well-trained crew could improve on this.

Below: An officer checks the sight setting on a M-1943 120mm mortar. The Soviet Army uses mortar fire to suppress enemy defensive positions prior to commencing an attack.

160mm M-160 Mortar

Weight: Travelling 3,241lb (1470kg); firing 2,866lb (1300kg).
Weight of projectile: HE 90·4lb (41kg).
Maximum range: 8,825yds (8070m).

This large mortar is a breech-loader, firing a 90lb (41kg) bomb to a maximum range of just over 5 miles. It was at one time widely used in motor rifle divisions but, as far as is known, it has now been withdrawn into reserve and is issued for specific operations only. The Soviet Army is known to consider it especially suitable for operation in mountainous country.

240mm M-240 Mortar

Weight of projectile: HE 220lb (100kg).

This enormous weapon is shrouded in mystery. It was first seen on a parade in Red Square in Moscow in November 1953, but the scale of issue has never been determined. Not only may it no longer be in service but, for all that is known about it, it may never even have entered service in the first place.

Below: An M-160 160mm mortar emits a large amount of "flash" during a night-firing practice. 2-3 rounds per minute can be fired to a maximum range of 8,825 yards (8,070m).

Below: This drawing shows the major characteristics of the M-240 240mm mortar. It is towed by a collar fixed to the muzzle and the wheels are permanently attached. The bomb weighs 220lb (100kg), more than the 180mm shell for the S-23 howitzer.

Below: One of the first pictures ever published of the 240mm super-heavy breechloading mortar. Judging by the rapid departure of the crews, firing must be an event of considerable drama.

Air Defence Weapons

Command of the airspace over their own forces is considered by the Soviets to be an essential factor in a successful offensive. Accordingly, the Soviet army has what is almost certainly the most comprehensive range of air

SA-2 Guideline Missile

Dimensions: Length 35ft 2in (10·7m) (varies with sub-type); diameter (boost) 27·5in (700mm), (missile) 21·6in (500mm); span (boost) 86·6in (2·2m), (missile) 66·9in (1·7m).
Launch weight: Typically 5,070lb (2300kg).
Range: Up to 31 miles (50km).

For uniformity the Western designations of this system are given, though after capture of large numbers by Israel from 1967 onwards there are few secrets left and the Soviet designation is reported to be V75SM, the missile alone being (in one version) V750 VK. This weapon system is quite normal in design, and it has for 20 years been perhaps the most widely used missile system of any kind in the world. It was planned as a general-purpose land-mobile system, though the complete system is very bulky and weighs over 100 tons. First put into production in about 1956, this system has ever since been subjected to updating and improvement. The original basic missile comprised a shapely weapon with a cruciform of cropped-delta wings towards the rear, a cruciform of small fixed nose fins and a third cruciform of powered control fins at the tail, all indexed in line. In tandem was a solid boost motor with four very large delta fins, again indexed in line, one opposite pair of which had trailing-edge controls for initial roll-stabilization and gathering into the guidance beam. The missile rode on a ZIL-157 hauled articulated trailer from which it was pulled backwards on to a large rotatable launcher incorporating many system-items and elevated to about 80° before firing, with blast deflector positioned at the rear. The boost burned for 4·5sec, the acid/kerosene sustainer then burning for a further 22sec. Apart from surveillance radars and Side Net heightfinders, the standard radar, called Fan Song by NATO, operates in A/B (E/F) or D/E(G) ▶

defence (AD) weapons of any army in the world. Close-in AD is provided by fire from small calibre weapons, including 12·7mm and 14·5mm machine-guns, ZU-23 multiple machine-guns and SA-7 man-portable missiles. Unit protection is provided by a mix of SA-9 and ZSU-23-4 mobile systems including SA-6 and SA-8 for both low and medium cover. Many of the Soviet AD weapons have been tested in combat in Vietnam or the Middle East and there can be no doubt that shortcomings have been identified by the Soviets and lessons learnt from these experiences. Several new systems are coming into service.

Bottom left: Polish Army technicians at work on the guidance bay of an SA-2 missile, designated V-750 by the Soviet Army.

Below: Although now somewhat elderly the SA-2 Guideline surface-to-air missile is still in large-scale service with the Soviet and Warsaw Pact forces. It has been modified repeatedly.

▶ bands, locked-on to the target to feed data to the computer van. The latter set up the launcher and, after liftoff, used a UHF link to pass steering commands to the missile, which had to be centred in the guidance beam within 6sec if it was not to fall out of control. The warhead was a 286·6lb (130kg) charge with an internally grooved heavy casing. Various impact, command and proximity fuses were used. Subsequently there have been too many modifications to follow, involving radar, guidance, control, warhead, fusing and, above all, ECCM. Very extensive combat experience in the Middle East and South East Asia forced numerous changes on top of an existing programme of new versions. The first externally evident change was introduction of cropped delta nose fins instead of rectangles. The latest family, first seen in 1967, have larger white-painted warheads (said to be nuclear), no nose fins and no boost control surfaces. Most effort has gone into the radars, called Fan Song A to G in seven distinct types with track-while-scan elements and a sawtooth-profile flapping Lewis scanner backed up by various parabolic dishes. Once exceeding 4,000, SA-2 launchers in the Soviet Union are rapidly running down. Other users included Afghanistan, Albania, Algeria, Bulgaria, China, Cuba, Czechoslovakia, Egypt, East Germany, Hungary, India, Iraq, North Korea, Libya, Mongolia, Poland, Romania, Syria, Vietnam and Yugoslavia. A naval version is SA-N-2.

Right: The air defence force possesses some 10,000 SAM launchers. many of which are still SA-2s. In addition, SA-2 serves in the army at Front and Army level; there are 18 in a regiment.

SA-3 Goa Missile

Dimensions: Length about 22ft (6·7m); diameter (boost) 27·6in (700mm), (missile) 18·1in (460mm); span (boost) 59in (1·5m), (missile) 48in (1.22m).
Launch weight: About 882lb (400kg).
Range: Up to 18 miles (29km).

The medium-altitude partner to SA-2, this equally aged system is widely used by the Soviet Ground Forces, Navy and many other countries. The missile is carried in pairs on ZIL-157 family tractors, mounted direct on the vehicle and not needing a trailer. The inclined ramps also serve as launchers. The same installation has been seen on three tracked chassis, while PVO-Strany now uses quad installations. When associated with the SA-2 this missile is fired from a power-rotated twin launcher elevated to 75°. Radars used in this system include P-15 Flat Face, a UHF acquisition set with superimposed parabolic aerials and range to about 155 miles (250km), and Low Blow, a target-tracking and missile-guidance radar of up to 53 miles (85km) range with mechanically scanned trough aerials at 45°. SA-3 and SA-2 batteries can also have early warning from P-12 Spoon Rest radars. SA-3 has a large tandem boost motor with giant rectangular fins which spread out through 90° at launch, a solid sustainer, fixed rear wings with ailerons on two opposite surfaces, and powered nose control fins. The warhead weighs 132lb (60kg). Details of guidance must be fully understood in the West, but have not been published. Terminal homing is provided, almost certainly by semi-active means, and Low Blow can steer up to two missiles simultaneously to the same target, with unspecified means of overcoming ECM. This missile is used by Cuba, Czechoslovakia, Egypt, East Germany, Hungary, India, Iraq, Libya, Peru, Poland, Soviet Union, Syria, Uganda, Vietnam, Yugoslavia and, in SA-N-1 form, several navies.

Right: The SA-3 Goa missile is also still in service in considerable numbers despite having been around for over 20 years. SA-3 serves with many armies and on Soviet Navy ships.

SA-4 Ganef Missile

Dimensions: Length 29ft 6in (9·0m); diameter $31\frac{1}{2}$in (800mm); span 102in (2·6m).
Launch weight: About 3,968lb (1800kg).
Range: To about 47 miles (75km).

First displayed in the Red Square parade on May Day 1964, this impressive long-range SAM is part of every Soviet Ground Forces combat army, to provide AA defence in great depth against targets at all speeds and altitudes. Mobile but not amphibious, the SA-4 system moves with the advancing forces in nine batteries each comprising three launch vehicles, one loading vehicle and one Pat Hand radar. Three of the batteries move forward about $6\frac{1}{2}$ miles (10km) behind the most forward elements, and the other batteries follow some $9\frac{1}{4}$ miles (15km) further back. All are ready to fire at all times. The basic missile has four solid boost motors and a kerosene-fuelled ramjet sustainer giving great speed and manoeuvrability to the limits of its considerable range. Missiles are put on targets initially by Long Track mobile surveillance radar (reported variously as operating in E-band and I-band and having very long range, most unlikely with I-band) and the widely used H-band Pat Hand provides command guidance and semi-active homing, the missile's receiver aerials being dipoles projecting ahead of the wings. It is persistently reported that this missile can also be used in the tactical surface-to-surface role, though how it is guided in this role has not been explained. It is typical of Soviet defence funding that a completely new tracked amphibious vehicle was developed to carry both the twin missiles ready for launch and the pair following close behind as reloads. Unlikely previous Soviet SAMs this missile has its fixed fins indexed at 45° to the moving wings. There is a large conventional warhead. SA-4 was deployed briefly in Egypt around 1970. It is standard with the Soviet Ground Forces and is gradually being issued to other Warsaw Pact armies beginning with East Germany and Czechoslovakia.

Right: The SA-4 is deployed at Army level in a SAM brigade comprising three battalions each of 9 launchers. There are 4 solid-fuel boosters, but the main engine is a ramjet.

Left: SA-4 Ganef missiles on their specially developed tracked launcher. The vehicle is said to be amphibious, but no pictures of it afloat have ever been published, and it would appear to be a hazardous undertaking, to say the least. The launch platform can be rotated through 360° and has a maximum elevation of some 70°. Missile range is 47 miles (75km).

SA-6 Gainful Missile

Dimensions: Length (with rocket nozzle) 20ft 4in (6·2m); diameter 13·2in (335mm); span (wings) 49in (1245mm), (tail) 60in (1524mm).
Launch weight: 1,213lb (550kg).
Range: To 37 miles (60km) against high-altitude target, half as much at low altitude.

Seen in Red Square on 7 November 1967, and many times since, this outstanding SAM system appeared to be misinterpreted by Western observers, even the ramjet inlet ducts merely being described as "prominent fairings". Suddenly in the Yom Kippur war in 1973 Israeli combat aircraft began to tumble out of the sky like ninepins, and SA-6 acquired an instant reputation for destroying its target no matter what the latter tried in the way of manoeuvres or ECM. The whole system is mobile, air-portable and amphibious, being mounted on modified PT-76 chassis. A fire unit comprises three vehicles each with triple launchers, a loading vehicle and a Straight Flush radar vehicle. Each Soviet Ground Force army deploys five such batteries, three keeping 3 miles (5km) behind the front line and the other two filling

Above: SA-6 surface-to-air missiles were revealed in this Egyptian military parade held to to mark the first anniversary of the Yom Kippur war. SA-6s were very effective against low-flying Israeli strike aircraft. The system comprises two vehicles: the launcher shown here and a second tracked vehicle mounting the Straight Flush search, acquisition and tracking radar.

Right: Initial boost is provided by a rocket motor, but when the fuel is exhausted the plenum chamber becomes the combustion chamber for a ramjet. The intake ducts can be seen.

the gaps 6 miles (10km) further back. Various radars, notably Long Track, provide early warning and preliminary target data. In Egypt the van-mounted P-15 Flat Face has been deployed with SA-6 units, both in parades and in the field. But the key guidance radar is Straight Flush, which has two major turret-mounted aerials and provides several functions. The top dish tracks the chosen target with a 1° H-band (7·7-8 GHz) pencil beam, and guidance commands are transmitted to the missile in I-band (8·5-9 GHz), with frequency agility over a wide spread. Terminal semi-active homing is CW, to which Israel in 1973 had no antidote except generally useless chaff. The missile is a beautiful design, with integral ram/rocket propulsion since urgently copied in the West. The solid boost motor accelerates the missile at about 20g to Mach 1·5, burns out and the nozzle is jettisoned. The case then becomes a ramjet with a larger nozzle, fed with ram air from the four ducts and with hot gas from a solid-fuel generator, which continues acceleration to a steady speed of about Mach 2·8. Control is by cruciform centrebody wings and fixed rear fins with ailerons for roll control and carrying command/beacon aerials. The 176lb (80kg) warhead normally has impact and proximity fuses, with IR fusing a source of argument in the West. Users include Bulgaria, Czechoslovakia, Egypt, Iraq, Libya, Mozambique, Poland, Soviet Union, Syria and Vietnam.

SA-7 Grail Missile

Dimensions: Length 53¼in (1·35m); diameter 2¾in (70mm).
Launch weight: (missile alone) 20·3lb (9·2kg).
Range: Up to 6¼ miles (10km).

Originally called Strela (arrow) in the West, this simple infantry weapon was originally very similar to the American Redeye, and suffered from all the latter's deficiencies. These included inability of the uncooled PbS IR seeker to lock on to any heat source other than the nozzle of a departing attacker—with the single exception of most helicopters which could be hit from the side or even ahead, if the jetpipe projected enough to give a target. The basic missile is a tube with dual-thrust solid motor, steered by canard fins. The operator merely aims the launch tube at the target with an open sight, takes the first pressure on the trigger, waits until the resulting red light turns green (indicating the seeker has locked on) and applies the full trigger pressure. The boost charge fires and burns out before the missile clears the tube. At a safe distance the sustainer ignites and accelerates the missile to about Mach 1·5. The 5·5lb (2·5kg) warhead has a smooth fragmentation casing and both graze and impact fuses. This is lethal only against small aircraft, and in the Yom Kippur war almost half the A-4s hit by SA-7s returned to base. Height limit is still widely given as 4,921ft (1500m), but in 1974 a Hunter over Oman was hit at 11,500ft (3505m) above ground level. An improved missile has been in production since 1972 with augmented propulsion, IR filter to screen out decoys, and much better guidance believed to house a cryogenic cooler in a prominent launcher nose ring. There are probably 50,000 missiles and nearly as many launchers, large numbers of them in the hands of terrorists all over the world. Users include Angola, Bulgaria, Cuba, Czechoslovakia, East Germany, Egypt, Ethiopia, Hungary, Iraq, North Korea, Kuwait, Libya, Mozambique, Peru, Philippines (Muslim guerrillas), Poland, Romania, Soviet Union, Syria, Vietnam and PDR of the Yemen. A small-ship version is SA-N-7.

Top right: The original SA-7 Grail, seen here in the hands of a Soviet artilleryman, is a somewhat limited weapon. A better version was put into production in 1972 which has an IR screen to filter out decoys, higher speed, and improved guidance. Many thousands of this simple and reasonably effective system are in service around the world, some of them with guerrillas and revolutionary movements.

Right: An SA-7 is launched from the rear hatch of a BMP APC. This picture shows how the booster charge has burn-out before the missile even left the the tube, with relatively little backblast. Once it is clear of the firer the sustainer motor will fire to accelerate the missile to about Mach 1·5. There is an SA-7 with every infantry section giving a carpet of air defence weapons across the battlefield.

SA-8 Gecko Missile

Dimensions: Length 10ft 6in (3·2m); diameter 8·25in (210mm); span 25·2in (640mm).
Launch weight: About 419lb (190kg).
Range: Probably up to about 8 miles (13km).

A surprise in the 7 November 1975 Red Square parade was a dozen completely new vehicles each carrying quadruple launchers for this advanced and highly mobile system which was rather incorrectly called "the Soviet Roland", and it was almost certainly derived from SA-N-4. Despite its great size the 6×6 amphibious vehicle is air-portable in an An-22, and carries missiles ready to fire. Inside the body, or hull, are an estimated eight further missiles, enough for two reloads. Towards the rear of the vehicle is the rotatable and elevating quad launcher, surmounted by a folding surveillance radar probably operating in F-band at under 4 GHz. Between this installation and the cab is a large guidance group comprising a central target-tracking radar, two missile guidance-beam radars, two command-link horns for gathering, an optical tracker and an LLLTV and telescopic sight. All the radars have flat-fronted Cassegrain aerials, the main set being a J-band (13-15 GHz) tracker with a range of about 15½ miles (25km). Each guidance aerial has a similar but smaller geometry, with limited azimuth movement; below each is the command link horn. After careful study semi-active radar homing has been judged unlikely and it is believed all SA-8 missiles have IR homing. The missile has small fixed tail fins, small nose canard controls, a radar beacon and external flare. The dual-thrust solid motor gives very high acceleration to a burn-out speed greater than Mach 2, the average speed in a typical interception being about Mach 1·5. It is believed missiles are fired in pairs, with very short time-interval, the left and right missile-tracking and command systems operating on different spreads with frequency-agility in the I-band to counter ECM and jamming by the target, with TV tracking as a back-up. The warhead weighs about 110lb (50kg) and has a proximity fuse. So far as is known SA-8 is used only by the Soviet Ground Forces, in extreme forward areas.

Right: An SA-8 with its quadruple missile launcher and self-contained on-board search, acquisition, tracking and guidance radars. Every motor rifle and tank division includes an air defence regiment with five batteries, each of five SA-8 vehicles.

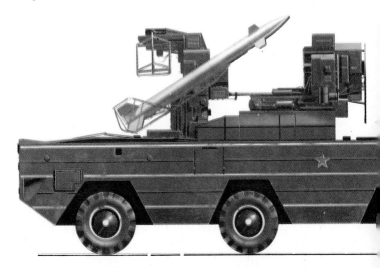

Below: These views illustrate
the major characteristics
of this interesting weapon
The 6-wheeled vehicle is very
large, and is amphibious. Each
pair of missiles has its guidance
antenna; the central dish is for
target tracking.

SA-9 Gaskin Missile

Dimensions: Length 71in (1·8m); diameter 4·33in (110mm); span (fins are not retractable) 11·8in (300mm).
Launch weight: 66lb (30kg).
Range: 4·35 miles (7km).

First seen in the November 1975 Red Square parade, installed in BRDM-2A amphibious scout cars, this light SAM system was at once assumed to use a missile similar to a scaled-up SA-7. In all examples so far seen the apparently simple vehicle carries little but four launch boxes (sometimes only the outer pair are fitted) on an elevating and rotating mount which for travelling can fold the boxes down on to the rear decking where protective grills can be clipped around the sides. There appears to be no radar, optical sight or other target acquisition or tracking system, though obviously one must be fitted. It is assumed that targets are acquired by radars in other vehicles which tell-off individual SA-9 operators by radio and may even slew the launcher automatically. Thereafter it is assumed that the operator sights visually and uses a small control panel with red/green lights to launch single, twin or all four missiles. In 1977 there were reports of BRDM-2A vehicles fitted with a new turret with a radar, almost certainly closely related to (or identical to) the Gun Dish used with the ZSU-23-4 Shilka AAA vehicle. Shilka has always been installed in the amphibious tracked PT-76 chassis, and this NBC-sealed vehicle would be ideal for SA-9 because it could carry missiles, radar and reload missile boxes whereas the four-wheeler is cramped. SA-9 is used by Warsaw Pact forces and Egypt, and is believed to be used by Syria, Iraq and possibly Iran. ▶

Right: An SA-9 vehicle on patrol. The four missile launcher tubes are mounted on a rotating platform and have an effective range of 4.35 miles (7km). There are 16 of these vehicles in a division adding to the already considerable air defences.

Below: Soviet crewmen in front of the BRDM-2 scout cars mounting the SA-9 air defence system. Detailed examination of photographs has so far failed to reveal any radar or other target acquisition system, though one must be fitted.

SA-9 Gaskins are used in platoons of four vehicles, operating very closely with ZSU-23-4 four-vehicle platoons. Their use is under the control of the ground force regiment. It is assumed that the SA-9s would be deployed between the first and second echelons of the regiment, and probably just behind the ZSU-23-4 guns, so that they could provide protection for both echelons without themselves being exposed to direct fire from enemy ground forces. Behind the SA-9 platoons would be the division's air defence regiment equipped with SA-6 Gainful or SA-8 Gecko, and this unit could give preliminary target information to the SA-9 platoons (or it could be obtained from ZSU-23-4 platoons).

All published war scenarios between NATO and the Warsaw Pact assume that it is the latter that invades the West. This might be expected to result in a vast concentration of SAMs in European NATO countries and very few in the east. The actual situation is the exact opposite. The Soviet Union almost certainly has more SAMs than the rest of the world put together.

Top right: Polish Army SA-9. In this picture only two launch tubes are fitted, and the front flaps on the tubes have been lowered, in preparation for firing. The window at the base of the mounting is for the aimer.

Right: Red Square parades remain one of the West's best sources of information on new Soviet weapons, where the the USSR shows just exactly what it wants to be seen. Here SA-9s are on parade followed by SA-8s. The grills on the side of the BRDM-2 are used to lock the boxes onto the rear decking when the mount is lowered into the travelling position. Aimer's observation windows are evident.

SA-11 Missile

Dimensions: Not known.
Weight: Not known.
Range: Maximum altitude 45,000ft (13,716m).

The Soviet Army's SA-11 air defence missile system has been under development for some years and is probably now on the verge of entering service. The system comprises four missiles mounted on a large box-like launcher which is in turn mounted on a tracked chassis. The SA-11 is so new that it has not yet been allocated a NATO reporting name. It is believed to have a maximum range of some 15 nautical miles (27,780m) and a maximum altitude of 45,000ft (13,716m). A large three-dimensional radar on its own tracked chassis is associated with SA-11, but it is suggested by some authorities that it can also be "netted-in" with the SA-6 system.

The Soviets have long stressed mobility as an advantage in offensive warfare, and the development of the SA-11 is in line with their desire to field highly mobile, low-level, all-weather air-defence systems.

Other missile systems are also believed to be under development, including SA-12, SA-13 and a "ZSU-X" gun-based air-defence system.

Below: An artist's impression of the new SA-11 system which is believed to be on the verge of entering service.

S-60
Towed Anti-Aircraft Gun

Weight: 4·42 tons (4500kg).
Length: (Travel) 27·88ft (8·5m).
Width: (Travel) 6·74ft (2·054m).
Elevation: −4° to +85°.
Traverse: 360°.
Projectile mass: (HE) 6·17lb (2·8kg).
Muzzle velocity: (HE) 3280ft/sec (1000m/sec).
Maximum range: (Horizontal) 13,123 yards (12,000m).
Effective range: (Vertical) 13,120ft (4000m).
Rate of fire: (Effective) 70rpm.

This is still the most widely used anti-aircraft (AA) weapon in use in the field armies, with a scale of 24 per division, although it is being replaced by either SA-6 Gainful or SA-8 Gecko. The towed gun is radar-controlled and can be used in either an anti-aircraft or anti-tank role.

The towed version of this gun is used by some 30 armies. A self-propelled version, mounting two guns in a large square turret, has been developed.

Right: 57mm S-60 AA gun deployed for action. This towed gun is still widely used, but is being replaced rapidly by self-propelled guns and missiles. Typical holdings have included 24 in tank and motor rifle divisions, and 18 in parachute divisions. Practical rate of fire is about 70 rounds per minute. There is a twin, self-propelled version: ZSU-57-2.

ZU-23
Towed Twin AA Gun

Combat weight: 0·93 tons (950kg)
Length: 15ft (4·57m).
Width: 6ft (1·83m).
Height: 6ft 11¾in (1·87m).
Ammunition: HEI, API.
Muzzle velocity: 3,182ft/s (970m/s).
Rate of fire: 800–1000 cyclic per barrel, 200 rounds per minute per barrel practical.
Effective range: AA 16,400ft (5000m); anti-tank 22,995ft (7000m).

The twin 23mm ZU-23 is in service throughout the Warsaw Pact. It is a fully automatic weapon with a high rate of fire, but lacks any provision for radar control, and can, therefore, only be used in clear weather conditions.

Ammunition is fed from two large, box-type magazines located outboard of the trunnions, each of which contains 50 rounds of ammunition in a belt. Maximum anti-aircraft range is 16,400ft (5000m), but the effective ceiling is 8,200ft (2500m).

These weapons are normally deployed in six-gun batteries, with one battery per motor-rifle and parachute regiment.

Four of these cannon, modified for water-cooling, are used in the ZSU-23-4 (see page 120), and a single-barrel towed version also exists, although it is not often seen. Like most Soviet weapons the ZU-23 has an anti-tank capability, firing an armour-piercing shell.

Above: The ZU-23 is widely used for low-level, unit air defence, with a battery of 6 in every tank and motor-rifle regiment.

ZSU-23-4 Quad Self-propelled AA Gun

Combat weight: 13·78 tons (14,000kg).
Length: 20ft 8in (6300mm).
Width: 9ft 8in (2950mm).
Height: (Radar stowed) 7ft 4½in (2250mm).
Engine: V-6 six-in-line water-cooled diesel, 240hp.
Armament: Quadruple ZU-23 23mm anti-aircraft, 1,000 rounds.
Speed: 27mph (44km/h).
Range: 162 miles (260km).
Armour: 10mm.

Extremely dangerous to aircraft out to a slant range of 6,600ft (2000m), the ZSU-23-4 is a neat package of firepower with its own microwave target-acquisition and fire-control radar, and crew of four in an NBC-sealed chassis derived from the amphibious PT-76. Each gun has a cyclic firing rate of 800 to 1,000rds/min, and with liquid-cooled barrels can actually sustain this rate. The crew of four comprise commander, driver, radar observer and gunner, and there is plenty of room in the large but thin-skinned turret. Gun travel is unrestricted in traverse, and from −7° to +80°. ▶

Above and right: ZSU-23-4 was produced by mounting a quadruple ZU-23 cannon on the chassis of the SA-6. All that was new was the turret and the valve-technology fire control and target acquisition radar. The result was one of the most devastating low-level AA systems in the world, and probably one of the cheapest! Practical rate of fire is 200rpm per barrel, fired in 50 round (per barrel) bursts; barrels are liquid cooled.

Above: GDR army crews at work on their ZSU-23-4 SP AA guns.
There are 4 of these weapons in every Soviet tank and motor rifle
regiment; 16 per division. They normally operate in pairs.

► First seen in 1955, this vehicle is used throughout Warsaw Pact armies where it is popularly named Shilka. ZSU-23-4 was tested under battle conditions in the 1973 Arab-Israeli War where it proved to be one of the most effective low-level defence systems. However, its radar suffers from "clutter" when trying to deal with targets below 200ft (60m).

The ZSU-23-4 is in many ways an archetypical piece of modern Soviet equipment, which marries a quadruple 23mm cannon derived from the well-proven ZU-23 to a Gainful chassis. Added to this is a valve-technology fire control and target acquisition system. These simple steps have produced a cheap weapon system which is very effective and much respected by any pilot who might have to fly against it.

ZSU-23-4 is issued on a scale of four to each motor rifle and tank regiment, giving 16 per division. They are used to protect columns on the line of march, and would normally be expected to operate in pairs. The practical rate of fire is about 200 rounds per minute per barrel, fired in 50 round (per barrel) bursts. A successor has been reported to be under development (ZSU-X), but it can be safely assumed that this weapon system will continue to serve with the Soviet Army for many years to come.

Right: A battery of ZSU-23-4 guns on a training exercise in the Siberian Military District. Note the infra-red searchlight on the commander's cupola, an unusual addition. Adverse weather and a poor road system mean that Soviet soldiers are able to cope with difficult conditions, and it would be unusual for the "going" in Western Europe to be as bad as it is in the USSR.

12.7mm DShK-38 Heavy Machine Gun

Weight: (Basic gun) 75lb (34kg).
Length overall: 62½in (1588mm).
Ammunition: All standard Soviet 12·7mm, in 50-round metal-link belt (in most installations fed from box).
Muzzle velocity: (API) 2,822ft/sec (860m/sec).
Effective range: (Horizontal) 1,640yds (1500m); (slant) 1,093yds (1000m).
Rate of fire: (Cyclic) 550–600rds/min.

This old gas-operated machine-gun is still used in great numbers, and in many applications. The basic design is well over 50 years old, but the Degtyarev-Shpagin model currently in service is the M-1938/46 of post-World War II vintage. Most DShK MGs used in land applications are carried on a two-wheel chassis, which increases the total weight to 368lb (167kg); the trail legs can be opened out to form a tall tripod for anti-aircraft use.

Perhaps the most widespread use of the DShK-38/46, however, is as the air defence weapon on armoured fighting vehicles, being used on all Soviet tanks from the T-54 to the present T-72. It is still an effective weapon, firing rate being 575 rounds per minute and effective range some 2,186 yards (2000m). In the earlier tank applications the commander had to emerge from the turret hatch to fire the gun, but in the latest tank there is full remote-control.

A new design of machine-gun has recently been identified on the latest production batch of T-72 MBTs. This has several marked similarities with the DShK-38/46 which indicate that it is almost certainly a Degtyarev design. The ammunition boxes on the side of the T-72 turret are slightly different from those for the DShK-38/46, which may be due to variations in the belt design, or could indicate a new calibre.

Above: The most widespread use of the 12·7mm DShK38 MG is as an air defence weapon on AFVs. Designed by Degtyarev, it fires 575 rounds per minute with an effective range of some 1500m.

It is not surprising that a military doctrine which allots such importance to the tank should seek to provide for sufficient means to destroy enemy tanks. As with most other armies the Soviets believe that the optimum anti-

RPG-7V AT Rocket Launcher

Weight firing: (Excluding projectile) 15·42lb (7kg).
Length: (Without projectile) 38½in (990mm).
Calibre of tube: 40mm.
Calibre of projectile: 85mm.
Mass of projectile: 4·95lb (2·25kg).
Muzzle velocity: 984ft/sec (300m/sec).
Effective range: (Moving target) 328 yards (300m).

Standard anti-armour weapon of Soviet infantry, the RPG-7V replaced an earlier weapon derived from the World War 2 German Panzerfaust which merely fired the hollow-charge projectile from a shoulder-rested tube. RPG-7V fires a new projectile which, a few metres beyond the muzzle, ignites an internal rocket to give shorter flight-time, flatter trajectory and better accuracy. The HEAT or HE warhead has improved fuzing, the HEAT round penetrating to 12·6in (320mm) of armour. The optical sight is frequently supplemented by the NSP-2 (IR) night sight. There is also a special folding version used by airborne troops; designated RPG-7D.

This type of anti-tank grenade has been developed as a direct result of the Soviet experiences in World War II, where battles frequently became so desperate that grenade-armed tank-killing parties were essential to success. Whether such tactics would stand any chance against modern tanks, especially those fitted with "Chobham-type" armour, is questionable. Recent reports from Afghanistan indicate that a new disposable, single-shot, man-portable anti-tank weapon has entered service. Designated RPG-75, it is either 73mm or 75mm calibre and has an effective range of 328 yards (300m).

Top right: The RPG-7V is still in service with the Soviet and other Warsaw Pact armies, that shown here being manned by soldiers of the East German Army Army. The rocket has a double means of impetus to protect the firer and improved performance.

Right: The Soviet Army considers lightweight anti-tank weapons to be effective if used in sufficient numbers and as part of an overall plan including heavier long-range weapons. Note the pack containing extra rounds.

tank weapon is another tank. Next best is an Anti-Tank Guided Weapon (ATGW) which combines long range, accuracy, destructive power and mobility. The current types (AT-4, -5 and -6) have greatly simplified control systems. Virtually all field guns have a secondary anti-tank capability in the direct-fire role. The M-1974 122mm SP, for example, has a HEAT shell with an effective anti-tank range of 1,094 yards (1000m). What is a little surprising is that old-fashioned anti-tank guns such as the SD-44 remain in service; their effectiveness against new types of armour on modern Western tanks can be marginal at best.

AT-2 Swatter Missile

Dimensions: Length 35·5in (902mm); diameter 5·9in (150mm); span 26·0in (660mm).
Launch weight: 55lb (25kg).
Range: 7,218ft (2200m) at 335mph (540km/h).

The first generation of Soviet anti-tank guided weapons (ATGW) was the AT-1 Snapper. This was much in evidence in the 1967 Middle East War and many examples were captured by Israel. It had four large cruciform wings, a single-charge solid motor and 11·5lb (5·25kg) hollow-charge warhead. It could penetrate some 13·8in (350mm) of armour.

The much more advanced AT-2 Swatter appeared some years later, and has also seen action in the Middle East and been captured by Israelis. It is carried on a quad launcher on the BRDM-1, and has four wings also in a cruciform, but rather smaller than in AT-1. All wings are fitted with control surfaces (elevons) with two carrying tracking flares. An internal

solid-fuel motor with oblique nozzles between the wings fires it off a launch rail of surprising size; interestingly, there is no high thrust booster. Behind a rather blunt hemispherical nose are two small fin-like projections.

AT-2 is command-guided by radio, which facilitates deployment from the various versions of the Mi-24 tactical helicopter and, it is believed, the AV-MF (Naval Air Force) Ka-25 ship-borne helicopter. Aerial applications are still thought to be of an interim nature, pending the entry of the AS-8 missile into full-scale service.

The one remaining puzzle is the nose, which suggests IR terminal homing, possibly in conjunction with the two small "foreplanes"; an IR seeker head is by no means impossible to combine with a hollow-charge head. The warhead has never been officially described in the West, but is said to penetrate 19·7in (500mm). Users include WP countries, Egypt and Syria.

Below: In the foreground is an AT-2 installation on a BRDM-1 amphibious scout-car. Note the blunt nose and the two fins behind it. The tracking flare can be seen on the left-hand missile attached to the trailing edge of wing. The two BRDM-1s in the background carry the AT-1, the first Soviet ATGW.

AT-3 Sagger Missile

Dimensions: Length 33·88in (860mm); diameter 4·68in (119mm); span 14·97in (380mm).
Launch weight: 24·9lb (11·3kg).
Range: 547 to 3,280yds (500 to 3000m) at average velocity of 394ft/sec (120m/sec).

During the Middle East war in October 1973 two-man teams of Egyptian infantry opened what looked like small suitcases and inflicted casualties on Israeli battle tanks the like of which had seldom been seen on any battlefield. Ever since, the little missile codenamed Sagger by NATO has been treated with great respect, though it is still a simple device with no tube launcher or any guidance other than optical sighting and wire command.

Called Malatyuka in the Soviet Union, it was first seen in a Moscow parade in May 1965. Since then it has been seen on BRDMs (six-round retractable launcher topped by armoured roof), BMP and BMD (single reloadable launcher above the main gun) and Czech SKOT (twin reloadable rear launcher). The Mi-24 Hind A helicopter can also carry this missile on its four outboard launchers, presumably firing from the hover or at low forward speeds. The missile is accelerated by a boost motor just behind the warhead with four oblique nozzles, and flies on a solid sustainer with jetevator TVC for steering. There are no aerodynamic controls, but the small wings can fold for infantry packaging. A tracking flare is attached beside the body, and it is claimed that an operator can steer to 3,281ft (1000m) with unaided eyesight, and to three times that distance with the magnifying optical sight. The Western estimated penetration of 15·75in (400mm) for the 6lb (2·72kg) warhead is almost certainly a considerable underestimate. Users include the WP armies and Afghanistan, Algeria, Angola, Egypt, Ethiopia, Iraq, Jugoslavia, Libya, Mozambique, Syria, Uganda and Vietnam, and probably at least five further countries.

Above: AT-3 anti-tank guided missiles mounted above the guns of BMP APCs. This missile can also be fired from a simple ground launcher and from helicopters. Called Malatyuka by the Soviet Army, its NATO name is Sagger.

Left: A Captain of Motor Rifle Troops stands in the commander's hatch of a BMP APC. Behind him is the barrel of the 73mm gun, with an AT-3 guided missile above it. At the front end of the missile is the conical cover of the shaped-charge warhead. Immediately behind that is the boost motor, and two of the four oblique nozzles are visible. Three of the four cruciform wings can be seen; these can be folded in certain installations, but there is no need for this on BMP. The tube above the lower wing is a tracking flare. Altogether, an effective combination.

129

AT-4 Spigot Missile

Launcher dimensions: Length 47·3in (1200mm); diameter 5·32in (135mm).
Launcher weight: 22 to 26lb (10 to 12kg) estimated.
Range: 2,187yds (2000m) estimated.

Code-named "Spigot" by NATO, AT-4 is a high-performance infantry missile fired from a tube, and generally similar to the Euromissile "Milan". The system has been in service with the Soviet and other Warsaw Pact armies for some seven years, but photographs have only recently become available in the West. Total system weight is 87·1lb (39·5kg) in the man-portable configuration. Control is Semi-Automatic Command Line-of-Sight (SACLOS) and guidance is by the usual means of a wire. Range is estimated at about 2,187yds (2000m), but may be as much as 2,735yds (2500m), although flight-time at such ranges may be a problem.

Right: The AT-4 possesses more than a passing resemblance to the Euromissile Milan ATGW. The design of the launcher enables the operator to remain under cover while it is fired; thereafter only the black tracking-head remains visible. Missiles are carried in their launch-tubes which are discarded after firing.

AT-5 Spandrel Missile

Launcher dimensions: Length 47·3in (1200mm); diameter 5·32in (135mm).
Launcher weight: 22 to 26lb (10 to 12kg) estimated.
Range: 2,187yds (2000m) estimated.

Allotted the NATO reporting name of Spandrel, this is the tube-launched system first seen on BRDM-2 armoured cars in the Red Square parade of 7 November 1977. Each vehicle has five tubes in a row, on a trainable mount amidships. The tube resembles that of Milan and has a blow-out front closure and flared tail through which passes the efflux from the boost charge. This blows the missile out prior to ignition of its own motor. Folding wings, SACLOS guidance via trailing wires and general similarity to Milan seem more than coincidental. The Group of Soviet Forces in Germany is thought to have replaced all its Swatter and Sagger missiles with Spandrel by 1979–80, a significant increase in its anti-tank capability.

Right and below right: The AT-5 entered service in the mid-1970s, mounted on the BRDM-2 scout vehicle. Five missiles are mounted in a row on a traversable platform, and guidance is Semi-Automatic Command Line-of-Sight (SACLOS) via trailing wires. Range is of the order of 2,187 yards (2000m).

AT-6 Spiral Missile

Range: 5 568 to 8,748yds (5000–8000m). No further specifications available.

This missile, code-named Spiral by NATO, is believed to be a large laser-guided weapon able to demolish any AFV. It is believed to be standard on the Hind-D helicopter and may also be fitted to the laser-equipped Soviet battle tanks. The suggestion that it is based on the SA-8 surface-to-air missile appears unlikely.

Small Arms

Soviet small arms are characterised by their simplicity, ease of manufacture and effectiveness. The AK-47, for example, has become a byword throughout the world and must almost certainly be the most widely used post-War assault rifle. It is now being replaced by a 5·45mm weapon—the AKS-74—which promises to repeat its success. A most

7.62mm PK GPMG

Weight of basic gun: (Bipod) 19·8lb (9·0kg); (tripod) 36·3lb (16·5kg).
Weight of ammunition box: With 100-round belt, 8·58lb (3·9kg); 200-rd belt, 17·6lb (8·0kg); 250-rd belt, 20·6lb (9·4kg).
Length: (Gun) 45·7in (1173mm); (on tripod) 49·5in (1270mm).
Ammunition: Soviet 7·62 rimmed Type 54R, propellant charge 3·11g.
Muzzle velocity: 2,755ft/sec (840m/sec).
Effective range: 1,093 yards (1,000m).
Rate of fire: (Cyclic) 650 rds/min.

Though a hotch-potch of other weapons (mostly the Kalashnikov AK-47), the PK family is an excellent series of weapons which can be described as the first Soviet GPMGs (general-purpose MGs). Unlike almost all other Soviet rifle-calibre weapons except the sniper's rifle it fires the long rimmed cartridge with over twice the propellant charge of the standard kind. It is a fully automatic gas-operated gun with Kalashnikov rotating bolt, Goryunov cartridge extractor and barrel-change, and Degtyarev feed system and trigger. The PKS is the PK on a light tripod for sustained or AA

7.62mm RPK LMG

Weight: With box magazine (loaded) 12·4lb (5·6kg), (unloaded) 11·1lb (5·0kg); with drum magazine (loaded) 15·0lb (6·8kg), (unloaded) 12·4lb (5·6kg).
Length overall: 41in (1040mm).
Ammunition: Standard M43 (M-1943).
Muzzle velocity: 2,411ft/sec (735m/sec).
Effective range: 874 yards (800m).
Rate of fire: (Cyclic) 600rds/min.

Standard Soviet LMG, the Kalashnikov RPK is essentially an AK-47 assault rifle with a longer and heavier barrel, bipod, different stock and two larger-capacity magazines, a 40-round curved box and 75-round drum. At any time regular AK or AKM magazines can be clipped on instead. Compared with the Degtyarev RPD of the immediate post-war era the RPK is much lighter and handier, cheaper and more versatile. Like the AK series it is gas-operated, with rotating bolt, and having selection for full or semi-automatic fire. It is often seen fitted with the NSP-2 (IR) night sight. There is no provision for changing the barrel which limits its sustained fire capability to about 80 rounds per minute. The magazine takes 40 rounds. There is also a 75-round drum magazine which is apparently used only in the early stages of battle.

imaginative weapon has recently appeared—the AGS-17 automatic grenade launcher—which will have a devastating effect upon infantry in the open. The basic user of all these weapons is the PBI (Poor Bloody Infantry) who take the brunt of any war. The Soviet infantryman is tough, undemanding and capable of great feats of endurance. He is not, however, superhuman and suffers from the constant turnover of conscripts, as well as from a somewhat uneven standard of leadership at junior levels in motor-rifle units. Although there are great incentives to stay in the Army it is known that only 2 per cent re-enlist.

firing. The PKT is a solenoid-operated version without sights, stock or trigger mechanism for use in armoured vehicles. The PKM is the latest service version with unfluted barrel and hinged butt rest, weighing only 8.39kg (18½lb); on a tripod it becomes the PKMS. The PKB has stock and trigger replaced by a butterfly trigger for pintle mounting on armoured vehicles (but the standard PK and PKM can be fired from, say, BMPs).

Left: The *Pulemyot Kalashnikova* (PK) is the first true general-purpose machine-gun to enter service with the Soviet Army. Designed by Kalashnikov it contains parts and ideas from a number of other weapons, but the result is an excellent weapon.

Below: A reconnaissance detachment on an M-72 motor-cycle. The sidecar is fitted with an RPK LMG fitted with a 40-round magazine.

7.62mm AK and AKM Assault Rifles

Weight: AK (loaded magazine) 10·58lb (4·8kg), (empty magazine) 9·47lb (4·3kg); AKM (loaded magazine) 8·0lb (3·64kg) (early version 8·4lb, 3·8kg), (empty magazine) 6·93lb (3·14kg) (early version 7·3lb, 3·31kg).
Length overall (no bayonet): AK-47 (either butt), 34·25in (870mm); AKM, 34·5in (876mm).
Ammunition: Standard M43 (M-1943).
Muzzle velocity: 2,345ft/sec (715m/sec).
Effective range: (semi-auto) 437yds (400m); (auto) 328yds (300m).
Rate of fire: Cyclic, 600rds/min, auto, 90rds/min, semi-auto, 40rds/min.

The Soviet Army has always understood the value of sheer volume of fire, particularly if it could be produced by not very highly trained troops firing simple weapons. During World War II they had seen and been impressed by the German MP 44, and as soon as the war was over they set out, assisted by captured German designers, to produce a similar weapon of their own. This led to the Avtomat-Kalashnikova assault rifle—the AK 47—an exceptional weapon in every respect. The AK 47 is accurate and sufficiently heavy to shoot well at automatic at the ranges likely to be required in modern war — up to 330 yards (300m) — without undue vibration.

Produced in greater quantity than any other modern small arm, the AK 47 and AKM can fairly be said to have set a new standard in infantry weapons. The original AK 47 came with a wooden stock or (for AFV crews, para-troopers and motorcyclists) a folding metal stock. It owed much to German ▶

Right: Signallers in support of a river-crossing laying field cable across the river to the bridge-head. They are armed with the AK-47 automatic rifle, which has probably been produced in far greater numbers than any other rifle in history.

Below: The AK-47 is worked by gas tapped from the barrel and driving a piston in a cylinder above the barrel. This piston takes with it the rotating bolt, the whole being thrust forward again by the return spring. It fires a 7·62mm cartridge which, despite popular opinion, is not interchangeable with the NATO round.

▶designs (and designers) and like them uses a short cartridge firing a stubby bullet. A gas-operated weapon with rotating bolt (which is often chrome-plated) it can readily be used by troops all over the world, of any standard of education, and gives extremely reliable results under the most adverse conditions. Versions with various designations have been produced in at least five countries and it is used in some 35 armies.

The present standard Soviet infantry small arm is the AKM, an amazingly light weapon making extensive use of plastics and metal stampings, and with a cyclic-rate reducer, compensator, and other improvements. Both rifles can be fitted with luminous sights or the NSP-2 infra-red (IR) sight. Another fitment is the new bayonet which doubles as a saw and as an insulated wire-cutter.

Altogether this has proved to be an excellent family of weapons, brilliantly effective for the job they were designed to do.

Top: The earliest versions of the AK-47 had wooden butts, then in the mid-1950s a fold-butt version appeared, principally for use by paratroops. It has also found much use with guerrillas, who appreciate its compactness, accuracy and reliability.

Above left: Soviet Army soldiers firing their AKMs during a river-crossing operation. The AKM is a development of the AK-47 with a number of improvements including a cyclic-rate reducer, compensator and extensive use of stampings and plastics.

Above right: A Soviet soldier with an AKM rifle. Weighing only 8·0lb (3·64kg) with a full magazine, it is 1·5lb (0·6kg) lighter than the current British 7·62mm L1A1 rifle, a significant difference. Its bayonet can be used as a wire-cutter and a saw.

5.45mm AKS-74 Assault Rifle

Weight: (With loaded magazine) 7·94lb (3·6kg).
Length: Not known.
Ammunition: 5·45mm.
Muzzle velocity: 2,854ft/sec (870m/sec).
Effective range: About 547yds (500m).

The success of the United States Armalite AR-15 (M-16) rifle firing the 5·56mm round in the 1960s led most armies to review their rifle designs. In the West some very curious weapons have appeared together with sound designs such as the British 4·85mm Individual Weapon, and there is intense competition to win the order for the next NATO standard rifle. The USSR appeared, however, to be satisfied with the AK series which gave excellent service both in the Warsaw Pact armies and with many revolutionary forces.

In the mid-1970s there was considerable curiosity in the West as to whether Soviet small arms designers would follow the tendency towards a smaller calibre, but for a long time there was no evidence of any activity. Then, suddenly in the usual Russian way, Soviet parachute troops appeared on a Moscow parade carrying a totally new weapon which had passed through design, tests, troop trials and into production without a word leaking to the West.

The rifle is designated AKS-74 and is of 5·45mm calibre, ie, slightly smaller than the US round. It is a Kalashnikov design and it is clearly based upon the AKM; indeed, it may even be a simple rebarrelled and modified version of the earlier weapon. The muzzle brake is reported to be very efficient, virtually eliminating recoil, and thus leading to a very accurate weapon, even when firing automatic. The plastic magazine and hollow butt indicate major efforts to save weight, which tend to be confirmed by the obvious ease with which it is carried.

Right: Soviet paratroops in Red Square carrying a folding-butt version of the AK-74 rifle, which looks almost like a toy in their hands. The bullet inflicts a particularly nasty wound.

7.62mm SVD Sniper Rifle

Weight (with PSO-1 sight):
(Loaded magazine) 9·95lb (4·52kg);
(empty magazine) 9·4lb (4·3kg).
Length (no bayonet): $48\frac{1}{4}$in (1225mm).
Ammunition: Long 7·62mm rimmed, Type 54R, 3·11g propellant charge.
Muzzle velocity: 2,725ft/sec (830m/sec).
Effective combat range: 1,420yds (1,300m).
Rate of fire, semi-auto: 20rds/min.

The Dragunov SVD sniper's rifle is a thoroughly modern, purpose-designed weapon, though it uses the same 54R ammunition as the old 1891/30 sniper's rifle and the RK series of GPMGs. It is reported that users are issued with selected batches of ammunition to increase accuracy. A gas-operated semi-automatic rifle, the SVD has the Kalashnikov rotating-bolt breech but a completely new trigger system, barrel and 10-round magazine. The muzzle has a flash suppressor and a recoil compensator to hold the barrel near the target. The PSO-1 sight is $14\frac{1}{2}$in (370mm) long, and comprises a ×4 optical telescope with rubber eyepiece, integral rangefinder, battery-powered reticle illuminator, and IR sighting for use at night.

Above: An infantry platoon on exercise in October 1978 armed with the new AK-74 5·45mm rifle. Designed by Kalashnikov this is almost certainly a rebarrelled and modified AKM.

Above: The 7·62mm Dragunov sniper's rifle is both accurate and easy to use. One of these is issued to every platoon in motor rifle units. and special types of ammunition are used to ensure the greatest possible accuracy.

The Soviet Army has always set great store by sniping and in World War II men were specially trained to spot German officers by their badges of rank and then shoot them. Today each motor rifle platoon holds an SVD rifle, with at least one man trained in its use. Special snipers' camouflage suits are also issued.

RKG-3M AT Hand Grenade

Weight: (Fuzed) 2·34lb (1070g).
Length: (Before firing) 14½in (362mm).
Diameter of head: 2·19in (55·6mm).
HE charge: 1¼lb (567g).
Fuze: Impact.
Typical range: Up to 22 yards (20m).
Armour penetration: 6·5in (165mm).

The standard hand-thrown anti-armour grenade of the Warsaw Pact forces is the RKG-3M, a stick-type weapon which is stabilised in flight by a fabric drogue. The warhead is of the High-Explosive Anti-Tank (HEAT) type, otherwise known as a "hollow-charge". The original RKG-3 has a steel conical liner in the warhead, but this has been replaced in the -3M by a more efficient copper liner; this change increased armour penetration from 5 to 6·5in (125 to 165mm).

The drogue is stowed in the handle but is ejected when the grenade is thrown, thus completing the arming process. The grenade should land as near to 90° to the armour plate of the target as possible to achieve maximum effect, and the drogue is designed to ensure that this happens.

RGD-5 Hand Grenade

Weight: (Fuzed) 0·68lb (310g).
Length: 4½in (114mm).
Diameter of body: 2¼in (56mm).
HE charge: 2·42oz (110g).
Fuze: 3—4sec delay.
Effective fragmentation radius: 27·3 yards (25m).

Probably the most widely used hand grenade of the Warsaw Pact forces, the RGD-5 comprises an HE charge in a serrated frag liner, enclosed in a body of thin sheet steel. The fuze is the same UZRG type used in earlier Soviet grenades, but the RGD-5 is much more compact and can be carried in greater quantity and thrown further. Normal throwing range is some 33 yards (30m).

30mm AGS-17 Plamya Automatic Grenade Launcher

Weight: 66 to 77lb (30 to 35kg) including tripod.
Ammunition: 28 to 30 rounds of 3 types—HEAT, anti-personnel, phosphorus.
Effective range: 765 to 874 yds (700 to 800m).

The Plamya ("flame") is a novel weapon which fires small grenades of three types. The first is an anti-tank round with a HEAT warhead. The second is an anti-personnel round with a warhead containing iron and plastic needles, which are fatal over a radius of 4·4 to 5·5yds (4 to 5m). Third, is a phosphorus round. The drum magazine contains some 28 to 30 grenades, and the cyclic rate of fire is about 50 to 100 rounds per minute. This is a most interesting concept, but the weight of the complete weapon is such that it can probably only be used in conjunction with a vehicle.

Top: The RKG-3M has a HEAT (shaped charge) warhead and has been known to penetrate 165mm of armour. This type of grenade was used in the Yom Kippur war with considerable success.

Centre: The RGD-5 hand grenade is a neat and easily handled weapon containing 110 grammes of TNT.

Bottom: The Plamya has only recently appeared and has no Western equivalent. The magazine contains some 30 grenades, which can be of 3 types: anti-tank, anti-personnel, or phosphorous. The anti-personnel round is particularly nasty.

Nuclear, Chemical and Biological Warfare Equipment

NBC warfare, sometimes referred to as CBR (chemical, biological, radiological), plays a central role in all Soviet

Means of Delivery

All Soviet artillery pieces of 122mm calibre and over can be used to deliver persistent and non-persistent chemical agents, but in practice, the most likely weapon for the delivery of non-persistent agents is the BM-21. The density of fire of this area saturation weapon makes it ideal for this purpose. A battery of six such weapons could deliver 240 chemical shells to a target area in a few seconds. Persistent agents would most likely be delivered by the long-range D-74 122mm and M-46 130mm guns. Agents of both types can be delivered by aerial bombs or spray tanks from FGA aircraft of the Tactical Air Armies. Chemical warheads might well be used together with conventional explosives to delude the defender.

Chemical Warfare Agents

The Soviet Union is known to hold stocks of several kinds of chemical warfare agents. These include:

Hydrogen cyanide compounds which cause rapid respiratory failure, but disperse very quickly. One contamination by this agent renders most types of gas mask and vehicle filter useless.

Nerve agents developed from insecticides by German scientists during the last war; the most important of these are known by code letters—GA(Tabun),

Right: It would appear that every soldier in the Soviet Army is issued with a respirator and chemical protection suits. This man is using a detector to assess contamination levels, on one of the regular exercises designed to make the troops thoroughly familiar with fighting in a chemical environment.

Left: Chemical defence troops in a routine exercise using an ARS-12U decontamination bowser. This has a 2500 litre tank mounted on a ZIL-157 chassis and is used to decontaminate weapons, equipment, vehicles and ground. Ten such vehicles are found in divisional chemical defence companies.

planning. The Soviet ground forces are better equipped than any other army for such warfare. Categorised by the Soviets as "weapons of mass destruction", this subject is under constant discussion in their military literature, with emphasis placed on at least nuclear and chemical operations being normal parts of modern warfare. Highest priority targets are the enemy's nuclear delivery means, followed by HQs, prepared defensive positions, troop concentrations and communications centres. Interestingly, the Soviets appear to restrict control of nuclear weapons exclusively to themselves, with no delegation whatsoever to their WP allies.

GB(Sarin), GD(Soman) and VX. Small amounts of these agents inhaled or absorbed through the skin cause malfunction of the nervous system and rapid death. These agents can be used in the persistent and non-persistent forms. Some nerve agents can be countered by antidotes or injections, but it is thought that the latest Soviet compounds may well prove difficult, if not impossible, to counter with present medicines.

Blistering Agents—developments of the mustard gas used so effectively in World War I. These are very persistent and produce incapacitating blisters and the vapour, if inhaled, causes death.

It is known that the Soviets maintain stocks of CW agents ready for use, and it is assumed that these would be issued to army formations as the result of a high-level political decision. All army units have the capability of delivering CW attacks, and divisional artillery recce is tasked to provide meteorological data for divisional staffs to plan their employment. In addition to this offensive capability, all army units and formations, unlike NATO armies, have integral chemical recce and defence elements for detection of contamination and marking of contaminated areas, and for mass decontamination of vehicles and personnel. Soldiers have individual NBC protective clothing and a decontamination kit, and all modern Soviet AFVs are capable of operating in a contaminated environment.

There are several types of Soviet NBC reconnaissance vehicles to detect and warn of contamination, at least 17 types of decontamination vehicle for vehicles, terrain and buildings, and nine types of mobile decontamination station for personnel and clothing. Some of these vehicles carry steam boilers whose output is automatically doped with an additive such as formaldehyde or ammonia. Others are tankers equipped with multiple sprays with special nozzle attachments, discharging alkali, other emulsions or fogs. Some use old aircraft engines as propulsion for the sprays (see below).

The BRDM-rkh reconnaissance vehicle is equipped with two sets of automatic emplacers for a total of 40 warning flags. The vehicle explores

Top right: Soviet and Warsaw Pact tactics and equipment are designed for both the conventional and the contaminated battlefield. These respirators and NBC suits (worn here by East German soldiers) are clumsy and hot to wear, and soldiers soon become heated, uncomfortable and tired. Even for the fittest and most practised troops a route march such as this would be very taxing and unpleasant.

Right: A closed-down T-62 tank drives slowly through a cleansing spray delivered by a TMS-65. This unique device comprises an old aviation turbojet mounted on a Ural-375 truck chassis. A trailer contains liquid decontaminant and this is injected into the jet pipe producing the fine spray shown here. With this simple, cheap machine the Soviets have obtained an effective cleanser, albeit one which is expensive on fuel. A larger version exists—the ARS-14— based on the ZIL-131 chassis.

the boundaries of an infected zone and marks the limits by the 40 bright flags, each automatically driven into the ground by a firing chamber and propulsion cartridge. The TMS-65 decontamination vehicle is used for the mass cleansing of vehicles and large items such as radars and missiles. The 6×6 Ural-375E chassis carries a VK-1F turbojet engine and operator cabin, with swivelling and elevation controls. Tanks on the chassis and a towed trailer supply jet fuel and additive decontaminants, delivered by the jet over a line of infected equipment (either the latter or the TMS-65 can be driven past the other).

Latest reports suggest that the Soviets have developed a gas-proof version of their field uniform. Once such a uniform is in general use, it will reduce considerably the impediments to the employment of chemical weapons on the battlefield. All Soviet soldiers carry an extremely effective kit of prophylactic antidotes which render harmless at least their own chemical agents, and probably anything the West has. It must be assumed, therefore, that in any major conflict the Soviet Ground Forces will use chemical weapons as a matter of course.

Above: A reconnaissance patrol with its BRDM-1rkh in the background. The yellow flag signifies that the area is dangerous and the soldier is assessing the precise degree of contamination using a special instrument. Exposure levels are dictated by regulations, but the Soviets permit far higher levels than the West.

Top left: These men are not surrendering, but are passing through a chemical decontamination shower. The Soviet Army's chemical defence measures are probably more practised and more effective than those of any other army. They certainly have decontamination equipment on a scale unparalleled anywhere else.

Bottom left: These Czech soldiers are members of a chemical reconnaissance and decontamination team. It is well known that the Soviet Army has chemical weapons and intends to use them; the position in the non-Soviet Warsaw Pact armies is not quite so clear. All armies, however, must be prepared for their use.

147

Engineering Equipment

Soviet Army planners realise that the proper execution of combined arms operations at the high tempo they envisage will require a very efficient performance of engineering tasks, so there are engineering capabilities

River Crossing

Assault bridging is provided by the MTU tank-launched bridges, by the TMM scissors bridge and by the PMP pontoon bridge. These enable Soviet forces to span virtually any type of water obstacle. In addition, however, there are GSP and PTS ferries to carry individual items of equipment across rivers. It must also be remembered that a very large proportion of Soviet AFVs can swim with little or no preparation, while most tanks can "schnorkel" when the conditions are right. There is even a specially developed inflatable lightweight pontoon bridge—the PVD-20—for use by the airborne forces. The heavy emphasis on river crossing capability expresses an emphasis on high-speed operations hardly consistent with Soviet claims that they are preparing to defend themselves against a NATO attack.

Above: A GSP heavy amphibious ferry transporting a T-54 across a river. It is formed from two vehicles and the cabs can just be seen between the two pontoons on the right. The left and right units are not interchangeable, which must lead to some practical difficulties. The GSP can carry a maximum load of 51·18 tons (52,000kg) which enables it to carry the T-10M heavy tank.

throughout the entire troop structure. Each Motor Rifle and Tank Regiment has an Engineer Company. Offensively, the engineers' prime function is to help in maintaining a speedy advance by clearing and maintaining routes, crossing obstacles and clearing mines. In the defence, engineers assist in the preparation of the defensive positions, lay minefields, and generally create obstacles to deny free movement to the enemy. Soviet Army engineers are well trained and have a variety of equipment, most of it good quality. Like most engineer corps Soviet engineers are also responsible for camouflage which is one aspect at which the general performance is not good.

Top: Another picture of the GSP ferry, this time in Czech Army service. The hull of the GSP is filled with plastic foam.

Above: A platoon of T-54 MBTs crossing a PMP bridge, which is being held in place by BMK-150 bridging boats. Each pontoon is carried on a KrAZ-255B 7½-ton truck which also launches it.

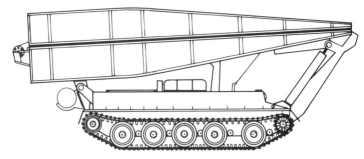

Top: MT-55 armoured bridgelayer serving most WP countries.

Above: The MT-55 launching its bridge; this operation takes 2-3 minutes. It can span 52·5ft (16m), takes a load of 49 tons (49,787kg).

Right: The Soviet Army's IMR (Combat Engineer Vehicle) clearing trees. This is based on the T-54/T-55 tank chassis, and the operator has an armoured cupola so that he is protected while working.

Obstacle Clearing

Large areas of destruction would be commonplace in nuclear war, and not all that unusual in conventional warfare. The IMR combat engineer tractor is designed to clear rubble and trees. 'Dozer blades can be fitted to virtually all tanks to supplement the efforts of standard 'dozer-tractors. Graders are available for road-making. In addition there are large quantities of engineering tools held in stock: power saws and drills, plus the associated generators. One area the Soviet Army is known to be interested in is the clearance of routes through devastated urban areas, a very likely place of combat in any future war in continental Europe.

Trenching

Trenching is not just of significance in defensive positions; even with their firm doctrine of attack the Soviets recognise the value of digging-in wherever possible. The BTM and MDK 2M are most effective rapid trenching machines. More conventional excavators are available for digging-in HQs, communication centres and the like, while an extensive range of explosive equipment gives a capability for rapid cratering and hole digging. If there is sufficient time weapons pits may be dug for guns, howitzers and heavy mortars, with further improvements to follow, giving shelter for the ammunition and crews. *continued* ▶

Above: All Soviet troops are trained in the fundamentals of mine warfare. but these combat engineers are specialists. They are formed into Mobile Obstacle Detachments (POZ) for rapid mine-clearing in the offence and mine-laying when on the defensive.

►Mine Laying

The ability to lay mines rapidly so as to thwart a counter-attack, or for protection on a likely line of enemy attack, is provided by the GMZ armoured tracked minelayer. Mines are also laid by hand-fed chutes. The Soviets have not yet demonstrated an ability to lay mines by artillery shells, or from helicopters, but this is probably only a matter of time.

Mine detectors are used widely. In addition to hand-held devices an induction-coil apparatus can be attached to the front of a VAZ469 vehicle for road clearing. The Soviets still place great reliance on the individual sapper with a prodding stick. In an assault, major reliance is placed upon ploughs (KMT) or a combination of roller and plough attached to tanks.

Engineer Support

One of the most important functions is engineer reconnaissance to provide comprehensive reports on the passability of advance routes, river crossings, and so on. To perform such tasks engineer reconnaissance patrols (known in the Soviet Army by the abbreviation "IRD") are formed, varying in strength from a section (squad) to a platoon. Other support tasks include power supply, water supply, construction of fortified positions, and movement support. The tasks of the engineers are endless.

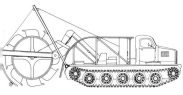

Left: Three specialised engineer vehicles for rapid digging. From left to right: MDK-2 ditcher/dozer; BAT tractor/dozer; BTM digging machine. All are based on the widely used AT-T gun tractor.

Above: The Soviet Army will carry out manual mine-clearance if there is no tactical alternative. These men are operating in two man teams: one has an old-fashioned "prodder", the other the IMP mine-detector which can locate tiny metal components.

Above: A new Soviet anti-personnel mine which has caused many casualties in Afghanistan and Israel. It can be airdropped from helicopters and is designed to maim rather than kill.

Left: Two soldiers wrestling with a PDM anti-landing mine. This is used in rivers and lakes to damage or disable landing-craft and amphibious vehicles.

Communications Equipment

Without adequate communications modern armies would quickly grind to a standstill; orders must be passed downwards, and information and requests upwards. The Soviet Army's concept of command is based on "top-down"

Command and Staff Nets

Soviet Army radio communications show some interesting differences from Western practice. The *command net* is used personally by the commander to pass his battle orders direct to his immediate subordinates, but can also be used to "skip" in order to command "two-down", eg, a division commander can issue orders direct to a battalion commander, etc. The *staff net* is used by the chief-of-staff to direct the rest of the staff at his own HQ, and also to keep the staff at higher and lower HQs informed of his commander's plans. Other nets are more conventional, with provision for liaison, coordination, logistics, traffic control, nuclear and chemical warnings, etc.

Soviet tactical HQs move very frequently, thus posing not only a problem for enemy intercept/DF, but also a considerable challenge to their own communicators. Divisional main command posts (CPs) move 1 to 3 times every 24 hours, leapfrogging with the alternate CP. At regimental level the moves of CPs are more frequent, but the distances are shorter. Such moves presuppose very efficient and reliable communications.

At the higher levels (division and rearwards) more reliance is placed upon radio-relay (microwave) and civilian trunk systems, but it would appear that, generally speaking, they are less complex than their Western counterparts and thus probably more reliable and survivable.

Below: An artillery battalion commander issuing orders from his rather inadequately camouflaged command-post.

Centre: Soldiers at an HQ erecting telescopic antenna masts on top of their communications vehicle.

control, which means only limited flexibility and initiative is allowed at the lower organisational levels. Their communications systems reflect this philosophy, while also taking into account the enemy's ability to interrupt and intercept electrical transmissions. In addition to their own command-and-control communications the Soviets devote considerable resources to electronic interception, direction-finding, and jamming, which will be directed against enemy radio nets, radio-relay systems (if practicable) and radars. The tactical emphasis on a fast-moving advance leads to a strong reliance on radio and all equipment is rugged, easy-to-use and highly mobile.

Above: A technical officer and his technicians watching anxiously as they test a bank of equipment.

Below: A motor-rifle officer with his radio operator.

Rear Services Equipment

At every level in the Soviet Army the Chief of Rear Services is responsible for the centralised planning of logistic support to achieve efficiency, economy and flexibility. One of the basic principles is that of "forward delivery", ie, each level of command is

Repair and Maintenance

Soviet military equipment is specifically designed to require the minimum possible maintenance in the field. Combat units carry little in the way of repair facilities, although at formation (ie, division) level there is considerable capacity for light repair. Soviet principles of operation dictate that damaged equipment is collected in assembly points, and the repair facilities are moved to these locations. Equipment is not evacuated rearwards, as a general rule, and only that which can be easily repaired will be touched; the rest will be ignored or cannibalised.

Medical Services

These work on the same basis as for vehicle repair, in that medical facilities will be moved to the area of greatest casualties, and not vice-versa. The existing Medical Services could never hope to deal with the mass casualties of nuclear war without a vast influx of civilian personnel and reservists, and even conventional war would stretch their capacity to the limit. The primary aim would be to return as many men to the battlefield as possible; sub-units would have first-aid orderlies, battalions dressing-stations, while the first echelon at which proper treatment could be given is division.

responsible for delivery forward to the next lower command level. When required, echelons can be bypassed to speed up the system, but this will be the exception rather than the rule. Contrary to popular opinion in Western armies, Soviet logistic planning is not dependent upon capturing materiel from their enemies, although anything which fell into their hands would obviously be a useful bonus. There is no doubt that the Soviet Army's logistic planning and units were rather weak in the first two decades after World War II. Strenuous efforts in the past 10 to 15 years have, however, completely altered that situation.

Below: A scene familiar to all soldiers as a GDR army crew recovers a ditched truck, using a Soviet KrAZ-255B (6x6).

Far left: A welder at work in a field workshop. Only quick and simple repair work is envisaged because of the time factor in a short, rapidly moving war. Any equipment requiring major repairs will probably be ditched or used as spares.

Left: Not an enviable job as a Soviet Army tank crew replaces a track on a T-55 in very cold conditions. Great emphasis is placed on operator repair and maintenance. All drivers and maintenance units are given set tasks to be completed at speci-fied intervals, and these are complied with meticulously. The maintenance problem is considerably eased by the essen-tial simplicity of the equipment.

Above: Fitting a schnorkel to a tank for deep wading. All WP tanks have this useful facility. although great care is required in selecting suitable sites, with good entrances and exits, and a firm river bed.

Transport

There are insufficient vehicles in the Soviet Army to meet its wartime needs and many lorries would be impressed from the civilian economy. However, since the same vehicles are used by farms and factories as are used by the army this would not pose too many problems. The basic army trucks are the ZIL 131 and the URAL 375, which have an excellent cross-country performance, aided by their automatic tyre deflating systems. Transport priorities —which are strictly enforced—are given to petrol and ammunition.

Fuel Supply

In such a vehicle-intensive organisation fuel supply is a major undertaking. A great deal of fuel is moved in road bowsers, especially near the front-line. Strategically, fuel is moved by train, and from the railhead to forward storage dumps road transport or field pipelines are used. The army's pipe-laying corps can lay up to 18·6 miles (30km) of pipe per day, with pumping stations every 6·2 to 7·4 miles (10 to 12km).

Above and right: Soviet Army field refuelling points are efficiently designed for rapid replenishment in fast offensives.

Left: Soviet Army vehicles are generally simple and effective. These four are typical of the many in service: UAZ-452A 4x4 ambulance (top); the standard field car—GAZ-69 $\frac{1}{2}$ tonne 4x4 (centre); MAZ-543 15-tonne 8x8 and ZIL-135 10-tonne 8x8 (bottom). All are made in the USSR.

Below: A field bakery. It is ironic that because of frequent poor harvests, the Soviet Army may well feed on grain supplied by its potential enemy!

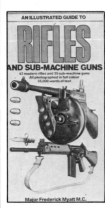

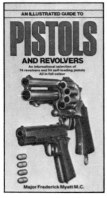